Also available at all good book stores

9781785316357

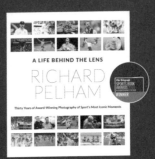

9781785315466

9781785317767

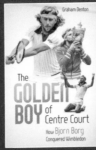

9781785317774

9781785313608

Wimbledon's
GREATEST
GAMES

Wimbledon's GREATEST GAMES

THE ALL ENGLAND CLUB'S FIFTY FINEST MATCHES

ABI SMITH

First published by Pitch Publishing, 2021

Pitch Publishing
A2 Yeoman Gate
Yeoman Way
Worthing
Sussex
BN13 3QZ
www.pitchpublishing.co.uk
info@pitchpublishing.co.uk

A CIP catalogue record is available for this book
from the British Library.

ISBN 978 1 78531 844 3

Typesetting and origination by Pitch Publishing
Printed and bound in India by Replika Press Pvt. Ltd.

Contents

To Lily, Henry & Tommy.
The court is all yours.

Acknowledgements

WHERE THERE is a will there is a way... never has this phrase been more profound. Covid-19, home-schooling, paper-rounds and childcare bubbles. This might not have been a never-ending struggle like a Mahut/Isner match, but it certainly felt like lockdown three was here to stay. Thank goodness therefore, for this escape into the world of Wimbledon.

I will always remember the excitement of receiving my first tennis racket so to begin, I must thank my parents for signing me up to take part in Coca-Cola awards and instilling in me a love for the game (over the net, remember Dad?). Chris, I hated your drop-shots but I still love you, so all is fair in love and tennis.

Thanks to TV director Simon Brooke, photographing legend Graeme McAlpine, the ever- helpful Sarah Parrott and former county player Robin Mayes who have helped enormously with their extensive tennis knowledge, expertise, and Wimbledon reference library. Robin, I look forward to seeing your vast collection of rackets one day soon!

Thanks to the behind-the-scenes coaching team who never let me dwell on a double-fault (writers anxiety) or an outrageous line-call (someone asking me to wear jeans) and to my trio of superstars who make me proud. Every. Single. Day.

Lastly, special thanks to Peter Butler, a neighbour who has become a dear friend and who continues to inspire us all. Jenny would be so proud.

Foreword

MY FIRST memory of watching Wimbledon is viewing the men's singles final of 1956 between Lew Hoad and Ken Rosewall on our tiny black and white Ferguson television set obtained a couple of years before for the coronation of Queen Elizabeth II.

I was captivated. Little could I imagine that in future years I would get to know both of those great players.

I started making my way to SW19 a year or two later, happy to roam around the outside courts and watch some of the greatest players the game has ever known begin to make their mark on the sport.

In due course via newspapers and local radio I found myself actually covering Wimbledon for BBC Radio. I endeavoured to have a go at radio commentary of the sport and soon learnt it was a mistake to try to describe every shot.

Then it was BBC Television and first the evening show which I co-presented with my old friend the late

Gerry Williams, who was certainly not a player of note himself, but knew more about the game of tennis than anyone. Fully ten years after we stopped doing that show Gerry and I were walking through the grounds of the All England Club when we were approached by two fairly elderly ladies. 'Looking forward to seeing you on the show tonight,' said one. 'We never miss it,' said the other.

How the memory can play tricks but Abi Smith has saved us the trouble of trying to recall some of the great moments of the Wimbledon championships down the years – she has done the work for us with her meticulous research. One of the matches she has picked out was the remarkable men's final of 1985 when a 17-year-old German came from nowhere to win the championship. In the final Boris Becker beat Kevin Curren of South Africa who had been the hot favourite after knocking out two former champions in John McEnroe and Jimmy Connors. There are many more stories of the great games. If you love tennis and Wimbledon in particular, you will be absorbed by this book.

Des Lynam OBE,
2021

Game, set and match

COMPILING A collection of the greatest games to have
ever been played on the grass courts of Wimbledon has
been, to some extent, the most challenging aspect of this
book. Various experts, former players, current players,
anthologies, tennis guidebooks, well-thumbed collections
and media gurus have been consulted. Hours of footage
have been examined and replayed to shouts of 'you can't
be serious, mum?!' as I take up position in front of the
TV to relive some of the best/most iconic/tremendous
tennis action that has been recorded. Strawberries have
been eaten, Pimm's has most definitely been drunk. All
in the name of research.

But the one (passing forehand) point I want to make,
before you start thumbing through the list and delving
into the action, is that this collection makes no reference
to order – the match that I have listed as number 1 is
only marked thus because it's the first game in the book.
There is no number one seeded match, no top three, no

out-and-out winner, nada. I won't profess to be anything more than a fan with a means to write, and therefore to rank them in any kind of order would be an insult to you the reader, the players and probably a ball girl or two. And whittling down thousands of matches across 144 years of play is even harder than returning a Sampras serve. You can do it (and I have), but there will always be balls that pass you by. So the games that I haven't included, well, it doesn't mean they still can't be on *your* list. And feel free to write about them.

What I would hope this book brings you, in a gentle overhead lob kind of way, and perhaps during a rain break from your own rallying, is a trip down memory lane: a collection of variety, of historical games; matches of significance, of delight; ones that brought thrills or upsets when they were played in the two weeks of summer.

Tennis teaches us about life ... And I have given this my best shot.

Maureen Connolly vs Louise Brough

Date: 5 July 1952
Score: 7-5, 6-3

'Here was the realm of my hopes, my fears,
my dreams, and as long as I live, I shall
be there in spirit, savouring the glory.'
Maureen Connolly

CHAMPIONS ARE sometimes known for their longevity in the world they play in, their years of domination cementing their success status. But not Maureen 'Little Mo' Connolly. Arguably* one of the greatest female players of all time, Mo was just 17 years old when she first came to Wimbledon, a journey that also marked her first ever trip to England. Her nickname, given to her when she was 11 years old by a San Diego sportswriter, was in reference to her powerful forehand and punishing backhand. After watching her hit a ball, he described her shots as having the same power as the big guns of the USS Missouri, known as the Big Mo.

The All England Club fell in love with her as soon as she arrived; she was young, passionate and poetic to watch, sailing through the tournament to reach the final on a warm July afternoon. Centre Court was packed. An all-American final between Mo and her opponent – three-time Wimbledon champion Louise Brough – meant that the crowd would be witnessing a teenager making her way for the first time onto the grass courts and competing with someone who was well acquainted with her surroundings. It wasn't so much young versus old – Brough was 29 years old, but would still go on to rank as world number one three years later; it was more that the crowds and commentators sensed that this was going to be a special moment for the little but mighty Mo.

Before the Championships, Mo had injured her shoulder in a practice game at Queen's Club and her coach, Eleanor 'Teach' Tennant, one of the top women's coaches at the time, wanted her to withdraw from the competition.

Seeking advice, Mo visited a local trainer who told her the slight pain in her shoulder was a bit of bursitis, a swelling to the joint, and that a simple ointment would help. But Tennant wanted a second opinion, and a chiropractor told the two that Mo had torn a muscle. The guidance was clear: Mo was not to play. If she did, not only would she be in a lot of pain, but it could potentially cause irrevocable long-term damage to her shoulder.

With that risk made clear and eager to protect her young protégé, Tennant informed the press that Mo would default the tournament that year because of her injury. But what an unforced error that turned out to be! Furious, Mo called her own press conference to announce not only that she would be competing at Wimbledon, but also that she had sacked Tennant. Some commentators thought this was a precocious act by a stubborn teenager, but her determination to play and prove them wrong was now her motivation. She might have come across at the time as a tough cookie who was not to be messed with, but years later she admitted that her argument with Tennant, on the eve of her first ever Wimbledon, had a profound effect on her psyche and left her 'emotionally torn'.

As they stepped out on to Centre Court all smiles, Mo was already harbouring the fighting spirit that had won her so many matches before this final.

The year before, at the US Championships in 1951, her opponent, Doris Hart, had called her a spoiled brat, but instead of intimidating Mo, it unleashed a killer instinct on court. Admitting that she had never hated anyone more in her life, Mo came back from four games down in both sets to win the match, revealing afterwards that she had 'turned on her [Doris] like a tiger'. Make no mistake; behind the sweet, smiley persona of someone so young was a ferocious and determined competitor. In fact, being angry with her opponent before a game, particularly if she got wind that a criticism had been made or she had been dismissed as an opponent, was like lighting a fuse and then giving that fuse a weapon in the shape of a tennis racket. Playing angry with an opponent suited Mo. Her anger turned into energy, focus and an overwhelming desire to punish.

So, in a way, you might want to feel a little for Louise Brough, who had hinted early in the Championships that such a big fuss had been made about Mo's shoulder injury that it would act as nothing more than a good excuse if she lost. When Mo heard about these quotes, she was fuming. This was going to be one explosive final. And given that both Mo and Louise had dropped just two sets across the whole tournament, the expectation that neither would be in the mood to tread lightly proved correct. This attitude from the American teen – who had readily admitted that she hated losing more than she liked winning – tested the reserve of the British crowd. We celebrated sportsmanship, fair play, good manners and decorum. Now Mo was paving the way for aggression, self-assurance and ruthlessness in women's tennis. Here was an assassin, armed with a big smile and a racket, and who played like she would never lose.

The final was indeed a hard-fought affair, with the action unyielding from both players in the first set before Mo broke Brough early in the second to secure a swift yet polished execution. Her shots carried weight rather than speed across the court, and her backhand punished Brough on more than one point. Her superiority was never in doubt; the accuracy of her groundstrokes was matched by their pace, and her volleying, which was still developing, was nothing short of devastating. It was remarkable for the crowds to comprehend that not only was this young teenager capable of causing such upset to a previous Wimbledon winner, but that she did so with such ease. As one sports reporter wrote at the time, 'This was as near to perfection in sport as one is likely to witness.'

No one at the time, other than her first coach, Wilbur Folsom, knew that she was a naturally left-handed player. Mo had originally visited Wilbur as a ball girl before picking up a tennis racket in her left hand, but she was told in no uncertain terms that no one had ever reached the top in tennis as a leftie. If she wanted to continue, she would have to learn to play right-handed. Perhaps it was this first 'unjust' hurdle that fuelled the spark in her competitive drive.

This win at Wimbledon marked the first of three consecutive Wimbledon titles, and the following year she became the first woman to achieve the Grand Slam. So an event that occurred in 1954, Mo fresh from celebrating her third consecutive win at W1A, was tragic in every sense. Little Mo was riding her horse near her home when it became spooked by a truck and her right leg was crushed. The accident meant she was unable to play again. She retired from international tennis that year and died, aged 34, of cancer. She had one of the shortest yet most significant tennis careers, but perhaps it was her spirit that was her greatest contribution. She showed no fear when she was on court, she took on champions and counter-punched all her rivals. There were no excuses when she played the game she loved, and she played with her mind, body and soul.

*Sorry, no argument; I have been told on good authority that she was the greatest.

2

Andre Agassi vs Goran Ivanišević

Date: 6 July 1992
Score: 6-7, 6-4, 6-4, 1-6, 6-4

'I value the trophies by what it took and what it took out of me. It's a reminder, a reminder of what we can overcome if we just refuse to quit.' Andre Agassi

THIS WAS the age of the big serve, the power players. There had been much discussion about how the serve was dominating the men's game and whether anybody could play against it. Enter Andre Agassi, the Las Vegas lad who always brought a bit of the razzle-dazzle of the iconic Vegas Strip to SW19 with his baseball caps, shaggy long hair and earrings. The antidote to the serve-volleyers like Boris Becker and Stefan Edberg, as well as new boys of the game, Goran Ivanišević and Pete Sampras, Andre was ready to shake up the tournament.

He had stayed away from Wimbledon since 1987, after losing to Henri Leconte in a match that was over in minutes and left a fuming Agassi ranting about how much he hated grass. Four years later he returned to the All England Club a changed player and reached the quarter-finals, eventually losing to David Wheaton. But now he was back with renewed vigour and confidence, which was handy as the journey to the final was not easy. Facing Boris Becker (the king of Centre Court at the time) in the quarter-finals was proof that his style of play was still valid against the mighty Becker serve.

'For me, it was very hard without a big serve, so I had to take my chances,' said Agassi. And take them he did. It was a five-set masterclass in perseverance and belief. Becker had reached the final of the Championship every year since 1988 and was now out. And not only that; for the first time since 1951, none of the top four seeds were in the semi-finals. But while Andre didn't have to face a high-ranking player in the next round, he had to face a highly sentimental one in the shape of John McEnroe. McEnroe was playing in his 200th major game and was hoping to reach his sixth Wimbledon final. But all hope of that was dashed when Agassi, on a gloriously sunny afternoon, beat him in straight sets in under two hours. And so to the final. This was Agassi's first Grand Slam Championship final on grass and, although the British tabloids cited his inability to get over the finish line, he was feeling empowered. Ivanišević was No. 8 seed and had knocked out Sampras in the semis, hitting a personal best of 36 aces. He was a big-serving left-hander. The night before the final, McEnroe rang Agassi to offer some advice from an old champ. 'He told me, "Listen, he will ace you a lot and have easy service games. But don't get discouraged, you'll have a few chances so stay positive,"' revealed Andre.

McEnroe, the master, had spoken and Agassi listened. He wasn't afraid to stand up to the power players with nothing more than his baseline style of play and quickness of eye and feet. But would it work against the 6ft 4in Croatian gunslinger? In a word, yes. Agassi, wearing the same cap he had worn throughout the Championships, in a nod to superstition, did face the battering aces as they came thick and fast, but he also took full advantage of the second serves and other scraps that were thrown his way. Seeded 12th and having lost all his previous encounters against the Croatian, he wasn't the favourite going into the match – but claimed that was a bonus.

'It freed me up to play, I didn't play scared, and it taught me to go out and strike clean.' After losing the first set, he saw the chances come his way in the second and third sets and he took them firmly with both hands, hitting hard backhands and dominant passing shots with passion and flair, delighting the Centre Court crowd. But then Ivanišević brought back those firing aces again in the fourth set and it was all Agassi could do to suck it up. But he had the advantage of serving first in the final set, which meant that if he could hold his serve it was Ivanišević who was under pressure to break and even the scores. It wasn't until 5-4 that the golden moment came for Agassi. He watched Ivanišević serve two double faults in a row and then miss the first serve on the next point. The crowd held their breath. Ivanišević pummelled over an ace. And then another unreturnable serve to level the scores at 30-30. But a return from Agassi that forced Ivanišević to hit a half-volley and then miss a passing shot meant the American underdog was now standing at match point. Ivanišević missed his first serve again. The crowd held their breath again. Would this match end on a double fault? Of course not. But if Agassi had heeded McEnroe's advice up to that point, to let the aces pass him by and move on, at match point he was going to give it his all. Ivanišević let out one of his epic power serves that came at Agassi with such force it would, at any other point of the game, have passed him by and been an ace. But not this time. 'I didn't want to have any regrets that I hadn't swung at a serve on match point, so I swung with all my might,' he revealed.

The return caught Ivanišević off balance and he played a volley right into the net. The match was over. Agassi, completely overcome with emotion, fell to the ground in tears, face down on the grass that he'd hated for so long – but which had now given him a Grand Slam title. Viva Las Vegas!

3

Roger Federer vs Andy Roddick

Date: 5 July 2009
Score: 5-7, 7-6, 7-6, 3-6, 16-14

'I had a feeling we would be there all summer long; that they would close the roof, people would sleep all night and wake up, and me and Andy would still be there, beards growing, holding serve.' Roger Federer

IF THERE was ever a man who was always bridesmaid to Roger Federer's bride, it was American Andy Roddick. Reaching the final of the Championship in 2004, 2005 and 2009, he lost out each time to Federer. It also happened in the 2006 US Open final, but we don't want to add salt to the wound.

The reason for us to include this match is the sportsmanship it personifies. Tennis is a mental game. All athletes have the technical ability to win, but it's how you thrive under pressure, in those critical moments, that can define you; the way you act in defeat and victory are the real indicators of your champion status – and quite possibly why the words from Rudyard Kipling's poem, 'If', are emblazoned across the frame of the doorway leading out to Centre Court. This counts far more than the silverware in your trophy cabinet. Even though Federer made history that day, earning his record 15th Grand Slam title, which saw him overtake Pete Sampras's record, he was gracious in victory. Knowing that the shared locker room wouldn't be the ideal place to celebrate when his defeated and deflated opponent was struggling, Federer motioned for his team to celebrate their historic win elsewhere. 'I thought that was considerate,' admitted Roddick. 'They should have been celebrating, but he kind of gave them one of these signs and they walked out and went about their business in another part of the All England Club.'

Federer was looking for his sixth Wimbledon title in seven years. With the legends of the game looking on from the Royal Box – Pete Sampras, Rod Laver, Björn Borg and John McEnroe, to name just a few – the pressure from the champions of yesteryear must have been suffocating.

The first time Federer and Roddick met in the final at Wimbledon in 2004, Federer was a set down but came back to win his second Singles title. The following year he beat Roddick in straight sets. Now it was the 2009 final, and while the years in between (against Nadal) had varied in their style, Federer knew he would effectively be going back in time to play Roddick, taking on more of a serve-and-volley duel. Roddick started as he meant to go on, hitting a 135mph ace on the first point of the match. He was playing the way that the press had labelled him – the guy that could serve but not much else. 'I am the most successful bad player ever,' he recalled. 'I used to hear a lot that all I could do was hit a serve, I couldn't volley, I couldn't hit a backhand, I don't return well ...'

But play he could, and the reserves and ability of Federer were sorely tested during that sun-drenched final. It would be an injustice to say that this was just another final for Federer and simply another chance to beat Roddick – he'd done it before, he could do it again. For several sustained moments in the match Roddick was the better player and it was Federer who was relying more on his serve, while his American opponent forced him to play harder and think harder than he ever had before. Roddick took the first set and the crowd went wild. He had to prove he was a worthy champion to the tough crowd after beating Andy Murray in the semi-final. If the people's champion was out, they wanted his victor to be the eventual winner of the tournament.

In the second set, Roddick led the tie-break 6-2, giving himself four consecutive set points. Given that two of those opportunities would be on his rocket serve, it seemed quite a good place to be in – who wouldn't want to be two sets up against the five-time champion? But almost as quickly as it was whispered that the reigning champion looked under pressure, Roddick buckled. The set point advantages kept disappearing in front of him and Federer fought back. After Roddick swatted a backhand volley wide, Federer won the next two points (making that six in a row) and levelled the scores at one set all.

'I thought the second set was obviously key to what came after, maybe being down two sets to love, the way Andy was serving, would have always been very difficult,' said Federer.

The third set saw more guts and determination from both players. If that second-set tie-break was playing on his mind (it would probably haunt him for years to come), Roddick didn't show it. The biggest enemy for a tennis player is the seed of doubt, and Roddick didn't seem to entertain that emotion as he fired back to bring the set to another tie-break – although it was a tie-break he ultimately didn't win.

In the fourth set Roddick knew he had to break in order to stay in the match and, on Federer's serve in the fourth game, he did just that, winning the game point with a beautifully executed backhand down the line. To take this tense final into a fifth set, he had to hold his serve and his nerve – he did both.

Into the fifth set they went and, with Federer serving first, the pressure was on the American. With neither man giving an inch, this was not for the faint-hearted; 4-4, 5-5, 6-6, 7-7, 8-8. Then Roddick earned himself a break point with a running backhand winner, but Federer swiftly served himself out of trouble.

As the great past champions looked on at the modern greats performing in front of them – like gods looking down from Mount Olympus – the play continued with both men not giving away an inch, slugging huge serves at each other with no chance to break. As it surpassed 20 games, the set made history by becoming the longest fifth set in a men's Grand Slam final (a record that had been set in France in 1927). Finally, in the 30th game, with Federer ahead 15-14 and Roddick to serve, the American mishit a forehand on the second deuce of the game and now Federer looked like he was about to break at the most crucial moment in the entire match. Roddick mishit a forehand and, all of a sudden, the four hours and 16 minutes of play came to an abrupt end. Federer, the now record-breaking champion, had done it. History was made. This was his sixth Wimbledon title in seven years and the longest Men's Singles final by the number of games played (77, in case you're asking).

Ever gracious in acknowledging the loser, the standing Centre Court crowd knew when to salute a player who had to serve to stay in the match ten times against the greatest player of all time. And ten times he had succeeded. It was just the 11th that broke the would-be champion's back. 'Sorry, Pete, I tried to hold him off,' sighed Roddick, as he walked off the court to the clapping crowd.

4

Serena Williams vs Venus Williams

Date: 6 July 2002
Score: 7-6, 6-3

'It's no fun losing, no matter who you lose to.'
Venus Williams

IF YOU are a bit of a history buff, you'll know that the first time two sisters competed against each other in the Singles final was back in 1884, which was also the year the first Ladies' event took place. Nineteen-year-old Maud Watson became the first ever Ladies' Wimbledon champion by beating her older sister, Lilian, 6-8, 6-3, 6-3. The Gentlemen's Singles tournament had been up and running for the previous seven years, but initial attempts to stage an event for ladies proved unsuccessful. And it nearly didn't happen in 1884 either; it was only two weeks before the Championships were due to begin that the Ladies' competition was entered into the Wimbledon programme. The decision was said to have been made as a hasty response to the London Athletic Club threatening to host a ladies' tournament at Stamford Bridge. Imagine! Wimbledon announced that the competition was open to 'all lady lawn-players' and there were 13 entrants in total, including the Watson sisters and future champion, Blanche Bingley. The final wasn't on the same scale as this sisterly battle. Maud and Lilian competed in white corsets and petticoats, and Maud's trophy, which she also won the following year, was a silver flower basket said to be worth 20 guineas. As with Venus and Serena, though, the competition was too tight to call initially, requiring a tie-break in the first set.

And so to the Venus and Serena final. This wasn't the first time they had played each other at the Championships; in 2000, the year Venus won her first Wimbledon title, she had beaten her younger sister in the semi-finals. But that was then and this was now, and the final carried with it the chance to be champion of one of the most prestigious tournaments in the world. The stakes were a lot higher. And if you've ever lost to your younger sister in the egg and spoon race in your last ever race at a school sports day (just me?) you might recognise a fraction of the emotion that bubbled under the surface of that grand final. The crowd were intrigued; would the sisters be chatty and friendly until the battle began? Would Serena release her traditional cry of 'Come on!' to motivate herself into punishing the opposition? Who would Daddy Williams cheer for? The crowd seemed more nervous than the siblings as the players came out onto court, the atmosphere strangely subdued yet full of anticipation as no one really knew what sort of awkward or potentially family-splitting match was about to be played. It soon became clear that Venus did not want to surrender her Wimbledon title and it became clearer still that Serena was not going to give it to her on a plate either.

There was no eye contact between the sisters at the toss of the coin at the net and Venus's changeover chair faced the baseline, her back to her sister. It was as close as you could get in the first set, with both sisters making their mark, regularly serving around the 100mph mark and trading powerful baseline forehands.

It was later in the second set that we saw the two competitors become predator and prey when Venus, suffering with a sore right shoulder, found that her service game was no longer going to match her sister's. After a half-hearted 67mph serve fluttered over the net, six inches wide, and more double faults, Venus was struggling. In the end, it came down to Serena to serve out the match, 5-3 up. The Championship point was won when Venus returned a serve into the net and, however frustrating that must have been, she ran to congratulate her sister at the net. That is what the crowd wanted to see; all is fair in love and war. The sisters were still talking to each other, no one was stropping off court. In a display of kilowatt smiles, big sis Venus looked like she was enjoying the moment as much as Serena was, reminding her sister to curtsy at the right time and enjoying the much-deserved standing ovation. Venus had lost the final and her No. 1 ranking to her little sister, but as one sports reporter commentated at the time, neither sister was going to 'go easy' just because their opponent was a familiar face. They discarded their sibling code of conduct and played with a ferocity normally reserved for others. Just two hours later the sisters were back on court, but this time on the same side, taking part in the Doubles final, which they went on to win against Virginia Ruano Pascual and Paola Suárez.

The Williams sisters would go on to play against each other competitively a further 30 times, and while this match wasn't seen as particularly epic in its drama, it raised a lot of questions about the competition in the women's game. Commentators were likening their dominance to the Pete Sampras years in the 90s, when no one could come close to matching his supremacy. The quality and power of the Williams sisters, the approaching retirement of Monica Seles and injuries to Lindsay Davenport and Martina Hingis meant that there were very few others who could match the prowess and power of the Williams sisters as they continued to meet in Grand Slam finals.

5

Björn Borg vs John McEnroe

Date: 5 July 1980
Score: 1-6, 7-5, 6-3, 6-7, 8-6

*I firmly belive that one of the hallmarks
of a champion – any champion – is
the ability to absorb losses and regain
confidence immediately.'*
John McEnroe

IT'S HARDLY surprising that the rivalry between these two players produced such an exciting and breathtaking final, and unsurprising that it features in our top 50 matches. It is rare for a Centre Court crowd to change allegiance for a player during a match, especially when it's the final stage – and, quite frankly, everybody has a favourite. But favoured player or not, the way in which this final was played – the fight and the comebacks, the relentless spirit and the emotion from the players – meant that both were worthy victors; the crowd, after watching the match, celebrated them equally.

Coming into the final hoping to secure his fifth Wimbledon title, Björn Borg was very familiar with the All England Club, who in turn enjoyed seeing the flair and unintimidated style of the Ice Man. Cool and calm on court, yet stylish and suave, he had been a worthy four-time Wimbledon champion. Having won two Grand Slam titles already that year, he was hoping for a Wimbledon and then US title to secure the Grand Slam full house. McEnroe was the opposite of his unobtrusive opponent. Passionate (read argumentative), determined (read explosive) and opinionated (read vocal), this young American had burst onto the tennis scene in a way that the mild-mannered stalwarts of the game hadn't seen before. He wasn't afraid to quarrel with officials but, importantly, had the talent and the ambition to back up his outbursts.

The final took place on a fairly overcast day with no rain predicted from the skies. However, the players received a torrent of boos from the normally good-mannered crowd as they walked out onto court. I say 'the players', but this theatrical display was very much aimed at the young American and a reaction to his 'Superbrat' nickname. The crowd were geared up for a good-versus-bad battle and were very much on the side of the golden Swede – English spectators especially weren't ready for this new style of player, the Johnny Rotten of tennis.

Still, the 21-year-old American wasn't fazed by the boos (although it probably was a little harsh, what with it being his first Wimbledon final and all) and, as if in answer to the cries, McEnroe won the first set with bursting confidence and unrivalled power. Borg, perhaps underestimating his opponent's ambition from the word go, was also a notoriously slow starter and it felt like he was half-heartedly returning balls in a warm-up stage (stretching his legs halfway through the opening set seemed to confirm this).

But when he faced three break points at 4-4 in the second set, something kicked into gear. It was time to show this young whippersnapper why he was the four-time Wimbledon champion. With a sudden surge of authority, Borg won the next five games. Now that the favourite had, to some extent, controlled the excitable pup, Borg continued to plough ahead and won the third set with relative ease. The crowd were continuing to show their support when he won points and disdain when he lost. And yet no one was expecting the fourth set to be the making of both men, the chance for them to see McEnroe display the relentless enthusiasm and ambition which, while previously seen as brattish and rude, were in fact the marks of a true champion. This was the set that would be talked about for years to come (case in point proved here) – or, more specifically, the tie-break that came to be known as the War of 18-16.

At 6-6, this would either be the tie-breaker that saw McEnroe live to play another set or it would be the tie-breaker that saw Borg crowned Wimbledon champion for the fifth time. And what a tie-breaker it was. For the next 34 points, both players showed why they were in the final of the greatest Championship on Earth. The speed of the groundstrokes was so fierce that both players launched themselves at the returns, Borg tumbling onto the ground, and then two shots later McEnroe sliding flat on his face. It was ferocious and compelling at the same time, a test of nerve and power, of skill and resilience.

Incredibly, McEnroe saved five match points while Borg himself fought off the same number of set points. Every well-disguised low-fast lob followed another, every approach beaten by a better topspin pass. The hushed crowd were on the edge of their seats; they hadn't been expecting these two world-class players to push their bodies and minds to the limits for this tie-break. Both seemed to grow bigger, stronger and more impressive with every shot, with experience being the only identifying difference. In the end, it was the more experienced Borg who gave the crowd the chance to exhale when a drop shot found the net and McEnroe won back the fourth set.

It looked like this was going to be the power surge of confidence that McEnroe needed to win the title. For Borg, losing that fourth set was surely enough to shatter the dream; he had just let slip seven match points, two on his serve, before the aforementioned five in the tie-break.

But how does a champion respond to defeat? By raising his game to the level of the gods.

In the fifth set, with McEnroe poised and running on confidence, Borg was down but not out. In a remarkable show of skill and determination, he fired up his serve and psychological reserve to lose only three points in his seven service games. McEnroe, so sure of a win only minutes ago when he fired off two winners to make Borg go love-30 in his service game, was now facing the runner-up prize. And while he managed to save two match points on his serve, he could only watch as a backhand passing shot flew away from him, carrying with it the dreams of becoming the new champion. As Borg fell to his knees in triumph, the Centre Court crowd rose to their feet in admiration. In just under four hours, they knew they had been the lucky ones – witnesses to a remarkable match. McEnroe had proved his worth to the judgemental All England Club and they had watched him battle with heart and soul. The crowds that had booed the brat on his debut final were now giving the man a standing ovation.

6

Althea Gibson vs Darlene Hard

Date: 6 July 1957
Score: 6-3, 6-2

'At last, at last!' Althea Gibson

SOME MATCHES played at Wimbledon are etched into people's minds as being the most historic, or the most memorable, or for being so breathtakingly outstanding that they can't believe they have witnessed such an athletic feat. The match that took place on a very hot July day in 1957 wasn't epic in its action, but it was quite remarkable in its significance. As the temperature rose to 100 degrees Fahrenheit, 17,000 fans dutifully made their way to Centre Court to take their seats. Very quickly, those without hats started fashioning head coverings from handkerchiefs or anything else they had to hand, to protect them from the sweltering English sun, while those in the commentary box, glad of the shade, looked on. All eyes turned to watch as Queen Elizabeth II made her way to the Royal Box, giving a wave to the crowds before taking her seat. This was the first time that the Queen was in attendance to present the winner with their trophy, so it was, by all accounts, a memorable occasion. She has only, in fact, attended Centre Court to present the trophy on three other occasions – in 1962, 1977 and 2010.

Then it was time for history to be made. Out onto court came the two lady finalists, walking side by side and clutching their huge bouquets of flowers. As they reached the net they turned around to the Royal Box and curtsied, both bowing their heads as they did so. For one of the finalists, Althea Gibson, it was more nerve-racking than the final she was about to take part in; she had only learnt the curtsy from 'watching the movies'.

Althea was raised on the tough streets of Harlem, one of the poorest parts of New York City, and was the first African American tennis player to win a Grand Slam title when she won the French Championship the previous year. Now it was time for her to make history by being the first black woman to hold aloft the winning trophy on the prestigious Wimbledon court. It was this match that was to propel her to international stardom, and it was this tournament that she had told her good friend and doubles partner, Angela Buxton, she was going to win. Having this level of certainty over her talent and ability could perhaps be quite off-putting to her opponents, but it was an attitude that she developed from learning to play on the streets of NYC, honing her aggressive style of play on the concrete courts. It was either play and win and therefore continue to play ... or go home.

Althea was raised in a small apartment block on West 143rd Street which, along with the adjoining cross-section avenues, was blocked off every afternoon to become a 'street play' area. It was there that she learnt to play tennis, picking up a bat and sponge rubber ball and hitting it to her friend, back and forth, back and forth. It was on this street court that she would spend most of her days, refusing to lose. She wasn't playing for entertainment; she was playing for a life away from poverty. But the colour of her skin prevented her from entering national events until previous Wimbledon champion, fellow American Alice Marble, who recognised talent when she saw it, fought for Althea to be recognised in the tennis world. She wrote an open letter to the United States Tennis Association denouncing their decision to ban her from the event, a decision that was then overturned. And so 29-year-old Althea travelled to England to take centre stage at the All England Club. She was so adamant she would win that she enlisted the help of her pal, Angela, to find her a dress for the ball after the tournament.

It would not prove to be an overambitious move. As the two finalists took to the blistering heat of the court on finals day, it was clear to everyone that Althea was easily the more dominant athlete. At 5ft 11in tall, she towered over her opponent, Darlene Hard, and the crowd, sensing they weren't going to see much of an upset to proceedings, took in the awe and athleticism of Althea as she dominated Centre Court. It was a straight-sets victory and one that was over quickly and efficiently.

Althea had made history by being the first African American Ladies' Singles champion and now the nerves were really getting to her as Queen Elizabeth came onto court to present her with the Venus Rosewater Dish. According to Althea years later, the Queen's first words to her were quintessentially English, a remark about the weather. She told Althea she must have been very hot and Althea was gracious in her response: 'Sure Madam, I hope it wasn't as hot up there for you.' You couldn't take the smile off her face as she posed for the photographers, with Darlene giving her grinning opponent a kiss on the cheek.

The American press was full of stories of this young black woman, raised in poverty, shaking hands with the Queen of England, but Althea didn't dwell on the momentous occasion; less than two hours later, she joined forces with Darlene to take on Mary Hawton and Thelma Long of Australia in the Doubles final. Althea won that trophy too, winning 6-2, 6-1 with Darlene. But still there was no time to relax; there was one more game to go – the Mixed Doubles final. Darlene went back to being Althea's opponent (keeping up at the back?) as she joined forces with her partner, Mervyn Rose, and took on Althea and her partner, Neale Fraser of Australia. It wasn't to be a hat-trick of wins for Althea as she and Neale lost, 4-6, 5-7, but by then it didn't matter. Althea had set out to do what she knew she would – win the Ladies' Singles trophy at the All England Championships and the respect of fans in the sport she loved. She showed the world that Wimbledon didn't care if you were black or white, rich or poor, only that you could play the game better than your opponent when it mattered most. And she did that.

Henri Cochet vs Bill Tilden

Date: 1 July 1927
Score: 2-6, 4-6, 7-5, 6-4, 6-3

'I made 17 points in a row, so I decided perhaps I should fight.' Henri Cochet

SEMI-FINAL MATCHES are quite often the graveyard of champions, those who are so close and yet so far from fulfilling a dream. The crowds for the semi-final match were of the impression that this was the way Henri Cochet's dreams would be heading as then two-time champion, Bill Tilden, seemed to be effortlessly cruising to victory and a third title. Tilden had played at Wimbledon only twice before (in 1920 and 1921) and had won both times, so if we are looking for patterns, his third attempt seemed to be right on track so far. But what happens when a champion crumbles? Or rather, what happens when the opponent who looked dead and buried suddenly springs back to life? We're glad you asked …

There was excitement in the build-up to the match between the Frenchman and the American; not because there would be an electrifying match as such, but because Tilden, who was considered one of the best tennis players of his era, was playing on the lawn courts of Wimbledon and everyone was keen to witness the legendary 'cannon ball' service. The arena around the court was packed and those who had climbed heights to secure a bird's-eye view were treated to probably one of the most exhilarating matches of all time. Tilden started his attacking game in the manner he had become known for, hitting powerful drives and speedy serves that quite literally made Cochet dive for cover. Here was a man who saw the possibility of winning with his powerful first stroke of every rally, be that on his service or a return of service.

Tilden won the first two sets comfortably, and when he went 5-1 up in the third set, it looked certain a lopsided American victory was on the cards. He had one more game to win to move into the final. When Cochet won his service game, Tilden knew that the power and force of his serves and drives should give him that final game and the match would be over. But what happened next is hard to explain. How do you put into words the way fortunes can be so completely and utterly overturned? How can you describe the fact that the Frenchman, who had looked completely out of his depth until that point, suddenly and without clear reason, started attacking every single shot that came at him? Perhaps calling him Henri Houdini would be more appropriate for this match as his spectacular escape from defeat can be likened to that of the famous escape artist himself.

Tilden was a tall, statuesque man, and Cochet was, in his own words, 'a much smaller Frenchman'. Where Tilden had power and baseline drives, Cochet had an instinctive side to his game. Where Tilden revelled in his strength and opened his shoulders in a full swing on his forehand and backhand, Cochet took a ball early on the bounce and seemed to use the power and speed against his opponent. Even in slicing, Tilden had a brutal way with the ball. And so perhaps it was no great change of fortune at all, and more a case that Cochet simply had an ability to wear down his opponent and then, like a tiger springing to life, pounce upon his prey and finish the job. It was about patience and belief – or, in Cochet's words, 'I don't think tennis should be played in a state of mental and physical fury. I prefer just to be mentally and physically aware; perhaps that is why I used to win so many matches in the fifth set.'

Cochet went on to win his first Wimbledon title when he beat Jean Borotra in the final in another five-set marathon. He went on to explain why he seemed to prefer losing the first two sets of any match he played. 'Probably why I lost to a few players not in my class early in a tournament was because their play did not stimulate me.'

Against Tilden, he certainly had now become aroused and, as Tilden served the first of his express-fire serves and went 15-love up, it was time for action. Cochet returned the next serve and won the point. He then went on to win the next 17 points in succession, bringing the third set back level at 5-5. Not only was 'Big Bill' shocked into playing an extra set when Cochet won the third, he was forced into another after that, thanks to the Frenchman's cool and collected tactics. Winning the third set had given Cochet the confidence to continue playing in this manner, slowly chipping away mentally and physically at Tilden, who was beginning to tire. In the fifth set, when Tilden led 3-2, there was perhaps a glimmer of hope in the American camp that he himself could make an extraordinary comeback into a game that had had his name on it until the tortoise suddenly overtook the hare. But it was not to be. Tilden didn't win another game that set. Cochet rammed home his late surge by winning the next four games to clinch victory.

One of the All England Club's most famous referees, F.R. Burrow, described the spectators as being in a state of shock at what they had just witnessed, being 'almost too spellbound to applaud'. Indeed, those lucky enough to be in attendance had witnessed a match that quite rightly deserves a mention in any list of the greatest games of all time. That it happened at Wimbledon and became a gem in our historical crown is even more special. It's worth noting that not only did Cochet win his first Wimbledon title that year, but he did so in the same style as in his semi-final, pulling off another improbable victory against the No. 3 seed, Borotra. The odds were stacked against him even more on this occasion. He was down six match points and faced being the runner-up at 5-2 when he awoke once more and went on to win the Championship, 4-6, 4-6, 6-3, 6-4, 7-5. If ever proof were needed that Wimbledon was where the magic happened, then no one need look further.

8

Arthur Ashe vs Jimmy Connors

Date: 5 July 1975
Score: 6-1, 6-1, 5-7, 6-4

'Connors wore an air of such arrogance, he regularly intimidated his opponents before he had hit a ball.' Arthur Ashe

DEFENDING CHAMPION Jimmy Connors was heading into this final as 11-2 favourite to win another title. As top seed, he welded a confidence with a slice of superiority as he progressed through the Championships. However, it hadn't been a completely smooth ride for him. A knee injury in the first round wasn't ideal, nor was getting a ticking-off from the Wimbledon committee after he complained about the state of the grass. 'This is bullsh*t,' he had remarked. 'How about paying less attention to what I do off court and more to what I do on it.'

Perhaps this wasn't aimed solely at the All England Club officials, but also towards his opponent in the final, fellow American Arthur Ashe. They had played each other only three times previously and Connors had been the victor on each occasion, but the tension between the two off court had grown, with Connors filing a libel suit against Ashe for calling him 'unpatriotic'. The remark had come after Connors had refused to play for his country in the Davis Cup, preferring instead to play in big-money, exhibition matches. It would therefore be fair to say that as the players waited in the corridor before coming out onto Centre Court, a sense of tension and contempt was volleying between them. If Ashe won the Wimbledon title, he would be the first black man to do so, a pivotal moment in the history of the Championship and for worldwide tennis. He was nine years older than Connors and many thought it was time he put his 'brat' younger opponent in his place. Taking advice the night before from his manager and fellow player and friend, Charlie Pasarell, Ashe decided to change tack slightly for the final. Instead of playing his usual attacking game, he would take the pace off the ball, keep his shots to Connors's forehand low, and use plenty of lobs to Connors's backhand side, a place where he was particularly vulnerable.

As they walked out onto Centre Court the stage was set. Ashe was wearing his Davis Cup tracksuit with USA across his chest in a not-so-subtle dig at Connors (who didn't have one because he wasn't on the team), while Connors wore a Sergio Tacchini top in the Italian national colours. Ashe stuck to his game plan perfectly, taking the sting out of Connors's powerful groundstrokes by repeatedly lobbing him after drawing him into the net.

Ashe's service game had also been considered in the late-night tactical talks before the final. He made sure he varied the pace and direction constantly. When Ashe went 5-1 up in the first set, it was clear his new strategies were working; the frustration from the reigning champion was obvious for all to see. When Connors served to try and stay in the first set, he missed a sitter to give Ashe a 0-30 point and the disbelief on his face was clear. Connors was no stranger to on-court emotional displays. He would regularly clutch his groin in a disruptive, suggestive manner, or wag his finger at opponents if they questioned line calls. On this occasion he covered his mouth with his hand, and was clearly in shock. He lost the first set.

The second set went pretty much the same way as the first; Ashe was dictating the game and not giving Connors chance to settle and play his own game. It was humiliating for Connors, and the Centre Court crowd, who were sensing a landslide victory in this all-American final and wanted the reigning champ at least to put up a bit of a fight, let their feelings be known. With Ashe leading 3-0, the grumblings got the better of some fans.

'Come on, Connors!' screamed one spectator. To which the now heavily harassed player replied, 'I'm trying, for Chrissake, I'm trying!'

When he lost the second set 6-1, Connors knew he had to dig deep. This was a man who hadn't dropped a single set en route to the final, who had annihilated Roscoe Tanner in the semi-finals, who thrived on pace and who seemed invincible on grass. And yet he hadn't been able to get into the game thanks to Ashe's perfect dictation of play. Unless something changed drastically, the third set would go the same way and a new champion would be crowned.

But the third set proved that there was still going to be a fight to the finish and Connors managed to hold his serve against four break points before clinching the set with one of his powerful forehand drives. When he went 3-0 up in the fourth set, it looked like the tide had turned, with Ashe reverting back to his natural game rather than the tactical style he had enforced earlier. But it was only a momentary slip. Regrouping after a break, Ashe levelled the score again by deploying the ideas he had executed so perfectly in the first two sets, sending low balls to Connors's forehand and slicing his serves wide to his backhand. When Connors lost his service game to give Ashe a 5-4 lead and a chance to serve for the title, the crowd held its breath.

Watching from directly opposite the Royal Box was that year's Ladies' Singles champion, Billie Jean King, who had clinched her sixth Wimbledon title the previous day. 'The match was one of the few men's finals I ever saw at Wimbledon live,' she later admitted. 'Without a doubt it was the match of Arthur's life.' This was it. Ashe was going to prove that a player most people thought of as invincible on court could be defeated. Three out of his four serves were so well executed that Connors, by now sensing he had been well and truly thrashed, could only find the net in return.

When it went to 40-15, Ashe finished the match in style by serving a slice out to Connors's backhand that was so feebly returned that the crowd were on their feet and cheering before Ashe had even secured the smash into the open court. The new champion whirled round to the players' box with fists in the air in triumph. It was a lesson for all, not just for the mighty Connors who had fallen very swiftly on his racket, but for the incredible way Ashe changed his whole style of play, his natural game, to become champion. As one commentator put it, it was the most remarkable achievement in the game. 'To go into the most important match of your life and adopt tactics that are completely contrary to your nature and style, is an extraordinary feat.'

It was indeed. There was no love lost between the finalists. They shook hands but didn't speak a word. Soon afterwards, Connors dropped his law suit against the new Wimbledon champion.

9

Ann Jones vs Billie Jean King

Date: 5 July 1969
Score: 3-6, 6-3, 6-2

*'It took 13 years to win. It was just a sense
of relief that the journey was finally over, as
well as happiness that I had won.'* Ann Jones

ANN AND Billie were at the peak of their rivalry when
they took to Centre Court to battle it out for the Ladies'
Singles title in the late summer of 1969. Billie had won
it before – for the previous three years, in fact – and had
beaten Ann 6-3, 6-4 two years previously in the 1967
final. But something felt different today; the crowd could
sense an upset was brewing. It was perhaps down to the
fact that Ann, in her semi-final match against No. 1
seed Margaret Court, taught a three-set lesson on how
to knuckle down and believe in yourself. But that was
Wednesday's game; now it was time to feed off that win
and focus once again as she faced the mighty King. For
the crowd at Wimbledon – and for those hanging around

the Centre Court, the viewers at home and those glued to the wireless – that dangerous emotion called 'hope' reared its ugly head. Could we dare to hope, after 13 years of patience and disappointment, that an English player would be crowned Wimbledon champion?

Well, you've got to give it to her, Ann could certainly talk the talk. She proclaimed to a British newspaper that she didn't believe reigning champion Billie was any better than she was, and it was just time that she stood up to her physically and mentally. But could she? At 30 years old, there weren't going to be many more years of opportunity left. After 13 years of trying, was she ready for the challenge ahead of her? And would she be the first left-handed player to do so? Apparently, that was a big thing in those days; being a southpaw wasn't seen as an advantage until the likes of Navratilova created the impression that being left-handed constituted a considerable advantage.

The final took place on a beautiful sunny Saturday, with the added excitement that one of our own, a British player, could be crowned champion. If Ann felt those nerves and the pressure, she didn't let it show. That the weight of the occasion didn't get to her too much was perhaps testament to the fact that she had played on Centre Court two years previously. As Ann and Billie strode out onto Centre Court, Ann clung to her flowers, rackets and white handbag as she turned to curtsy to another

Ann(e), the Princess Royal, who had taken the place of the Queen who was ill. This was the first Championship to take place after the death of Princess Marina. Might fate be playing a hand and could the Royal Anne be a good-luck mascot for the tennis Ann? See what we mean about having hope? You really do clutch at straws!

If Ann's semi-final was a game full of tension and excellent tennis – and had been, according to the player, 'a principal achievement of her career' – could she go one step further and overachieve in the final? The crowd certainly believed she could; the level of cheering and excitement on Centre Court was high. Some of the spectators had been lucky enough to watch her in the semi-final, where they witnessed a new Ann, an Ann that attacked, didn't rely on her baseline strokes and was confident enough to take risks and go for winners.

Her serve and volley was now on top form. Her career had seen her as a steady if unexciting player, but now there was a fight about her game. As a player who confessed she was 'happier playing on court No. 15 than Centre Court', she was now fed up of being patient, she wanted to win. It was a now-or-never moment, but it looked like a Wimbledon victory would elude her as Billie broke her serve in the first set. Ann was looking weary. She was limping from a strained thigh muscle, a legacy of her epic semi-final, and it soon became clear that she was struggling, finding it difficult to get into her rhythm and to volley as quickly as she had against Margaret.

The crowd feared the worst. But all was not lost … She had lost the first set to Margaret after an epic 10-12 defeat, so she knew she could do it again. She'd had enough of wanting at Wimbledon in the final stages; this was her match. As they began the second set, the crowd and commentators immediately sensed a shift in power. Ann started winning valuable points and there was little doubt that the rousing cheering and shouts from the crowd encouraged Ann and helped her focus on the attack. She broke Billie's serve, held hers and went on to win the second set easily.

With the crowd gathering and viewers at home glued to the TV sets (Roger Moore was watching the match in between filming *The Saint*, while The Beatles famously stopped one of their dubbing sessions to listen to the match), the tension was mounting.

The trophy was in her sights now, and the previously slow and steady Ann now looked dangerous. In fact, she looked like a winner. Ann was slicing her backhands and winning vital points while Billie kept making the mistake of hitting her volleys low and returnable. Ann was edging closer. And then, at 16 minutes past three, the dream came true and, after over a decade of not winning a single thing at the All England Club, Ann was the new Ladies' Singles champion. It was a double fault that gave her the victory, but no one cared. Not even a momentarily frustrated Billie seemed to be hung up on giving away the Championship point, climbing over the net to embrace a delighted Ann. The Centre Court crowd erupted in deafening cheers and everyone rose from their seats to clap and cheer their new champion. It seemed like the spectators too had been on the long journey and were pleased the wait was over. And now that Ann had her hands on the Venus Rosewater Dish, she wasn't going to give it up easily. But not in the sense you might think. She didn't return to Wimbledon the following year as reigning champion, nor did she play in many more matches at all after this victory, deciding instead to retire and start a family. No, Ann literally wasn't going to give up the trophy easily. As she came off court she was asked to hand over the Venus Rosewater Dish so it could be taken for engraving, but she wasn't having that – it had taken her long enough to get her hands on it! She quickly went into the dressing rooms and locked herself in the toilet with it. 'It's taken me so long to win it, I thought to myself, I'm hanging on to it. I wanted to sit and look at it for half an hour.'

Well, who can blame her?

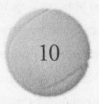

10

Rod Laver vs John Newcombe

Date: 5 July 1969
Score: 6-4, 5-7, 6-4, 6-4

*'You've only got to win seven matches, not
120 of them. If I won my matches, then I
would see who I needed to play.'* Rod Laver

THEY SAY a champion is determined not by their
number of wins but by how many times they come
back after a defeat. By how well they can cope with
the pressure. By how much hunger they have for each
point. For Rod Laver, entering the Championships in the
summer of 1969, this was going to be a test of all of those
factors and more. He had won the first two major titles of
the Grand Slam that year (Australia and French) and was
looking to continue his success at the All England Club,
the third hurdle. If he won, only the US title would stand
between him and the completion of his second historic
Grand Slam. Even if the quietly confident spectators at
Wimbledon didn't think Rod would struggle to win the

title, the pressure he was putting himself under was an excess burden he struggled to carry in the early rounds. In fact, the dream was nearly all over in the second round when he went two sets down on Court No. 4 to Premjit Lall, a relatively unknown scholar. As the crowds started to gather in the aisles between the outside courts to get a glimpse of the No. 1 seed, the tension mounted. Here was the reigning champion, facing defeat, struggling, trying and yet failing to get back into a match that should have been an easy warm-up for him. Having lost the first set 6-3, and the second set 6-4, he was now 3-2 in the third set and the assembled throng of tennis fans were in a state of shock.

As word spread that the mighty Laver was in trouble, the assembled crowds voiced their encouragement and cheered their support. It might not have been the reason for his eventual win, but it certainly gave him his fight back – that and the fact that Lall became the victim of cramp and spent a furious few minutes rubbing his leg in vain. He was injured and didn't win another game in the entire match, losing 6-3, 6-4, 3-6, 0-6, 0-6. Perhaps fate had played a hand in Laver's victory, but his renewed confidence ultimately won him the game. And that wasn't his only test in his journey to reach the final; in the semi-final he faced the 1968 US Open champion, Arthur Ashe, a player who would later become the 1975 Wimbledon champion.

'He led 5-0 in the first set and he was serving aces, hitting winners, hitting return of serves for winners,' Laver admitted. 'For those five games he didn't make an error and I said to myself, "He can't keep this up, he can't hit like this all the time otherwise I'm going to lose for sure."'

It was this grip on his self-belief and perseverance in a situation in which others might have crumbled that gave him the strength to bide his time as Ashe performed around him. And bide his time he did. After 90 minutes Laver had fought back, winning the last nine games and seeing off the future champion in the final set in just 14 minutes. Now he was going into his sixth Wimbledon final and would be facing the 1967 champion, John Newcombe. Having lost to Newcombe only a few weeks before in the semi-final at Queen's Club, Laver knew that the 25-year-old was hungry for another Wimbledon title. It was just a question of tactics. Laver's style was disciplined and controlled, a leftie who combined aggressive groundstrokes with speedy reactions. Newcombe, the 'Newk', was a heavy-hitting server who made sure he did his homework on all the players that were to cross his path. He once said that 45 minutes before each match he would visualise a dress rehearsal of how the game was going to pan out, which he believed gave him a clear mental advantage over a lot of players. As the Australian duo entered Centre Court to a resounding cacophony of applause, it was clear that the majority would like to see the older Aussie lift the trophy in a nod to his Grand Slam journey. Laver's only strategy was to focus on Newcombe's backhand – which was, on balance, a little worse than his forehand – and to keep him moving around the court so that he didn't have time to dictate the game.

At one set all, Newcombe was serving at 4-2 when Laver made the shot that changed the direction of the game. After a beautiful return to give him a 0-15 lead, Laver then chipped a ball sharply across court, a response to Newcombe's sharply angled cross-volley that he believed gave him advantage to most of Laver's next shots. But it didn't. 'It was just out of my reach and touched the outside of the line. I remember as I watched, I turned and gave Rod a nod of my head, acknowledging the greatness of the shot.'

It was an instinctive shot but it gave Laver the chance to get back into that set. And get back into it he did. Every shot was thought about and considered by each player. Newcombe played a lot of low shots to Laver's forehand volley, which meant Laver was forced to play safe returns, while his high lobs also required a degree of thought rather than reaction because of the small-headed rackets the players were using. The ball would have to bounce before a return shot was played, otherwise the players risked making errors volleying it back in the air.

Both Australians were capable, but which would triumph? The mighty Laver. Laver's chipped backhand cross-court shot in the third set that left Newcombe stunned had been the turning point and would be forever etched in Newcombe's memory. Laver recalled, 'He said later to me, "How did you even think about that shot?" because he thought I was going to hit with a top-spin backhand down the line, but I didn't'.

Very rarely is one such shot the focus of a final, but in this case, when Newcombe had all the chances to win, such hits really are pivotal. Winning in four sets, Laver was able to continue on his Grand Slam journey and went on to win the US Open that year, achieving the dream. Four majors won in a year – twice. We'll just leave that here.

11

Jamie Murray and Jelena Janković vs Jonas Björkman and Alicia Molik

Date: 8 July 2007
Score: 6-4, 3-6, 6-1

'I was motivating him every time. When it was break point I was telling him, "Hit a good return because you know you are gonna get many more kisses."' Jelena Janković

A FAIRLY heavy expectation falls onto your shoulders when you are closing the Championships by playing the last match of the tournament on Centre Court. Not only that, but you've also just followed the epic Men's Singles contest. And not only that, but all of Britain is hoping you are going to be the player to celebrate after not seeing a Briton win a title for 20 years. Oh, and your younger brother is British No. 1 Andy Murray, and you've never previously played at a Grand Slam event with your current partner. Well, actually, this tournament is the first time you've ever paired up. You haven't even practised together and she only said yes to being your team-mate the day before the tournament started. You'd spare a thought for Jamie Murray in these circumstances, wouldn't you?

While it was true that the Centre Court crowd would be leaving their seats after watching the epic Men's Singles final, for many spectators it was only a quick leg stretch, Pimm's refill and comfort break before heading back to their seats to watch Jamie and his Serbian partner, Jelena, take to the court. When asked back in March about his chances of claiming a Grand Slam trophy before his brother, Andy, the older Scot replied that the odds would be pretty good if anyone wanted to place a bet. If only we were betting people, of course. But to achieve this, finding a partner to play with would be top of the 'to-do' list – and, preferably, not just a day before the start of the Championships ...

No. 3 seed Jelena Janković had lost out in the fourth round of the Ladies' Singles to the eventual winner, Marion Bartoli, but was a self-confessed doubles novice. In fact, she hadn't contemplated playing doubles until Jamie's agent made contact with her before the tournament. Jamie had heard of Jelena, but she was only aware of one tennis-playing Murray at that time. She therefore wasn't sure what to make of the proposition when she heard that Andy's older brother wondered if she would be his team-mate, the day before the tournament began. With only 20 minutes of practice play together before their first match, they went out onto court that day and very nearly lost. But they didn't and then something clicked; the infectious positive attitude of Jelena and the long reach and power of the Scot had the makings of a dream team. Sometimes contrasting personalities are considered de rigueur in doubles, but here were two people that were as one.

As they advanced through the Championships, they grew in confidence, style and clout. They came out onto Centre Court at 6.30pm that evening and the crowd were in the mood for a show. Never mind that the Federer-Nadal final had been beautiful to watch; this was the moment when a British hopeful could become a British champion and it was the perfect ending to the Championships. They were greeted like the winners, before a shot had been played. The smiles and the easy way they had with each other were testament to their relaxed style of play and it was little wonder that the press and commentators during the past two weeks had dubbed them 'an item', labelling them 'giggling lovebirds' and picking up on the sparks they shared during their press conferences. And, of course, the fact that there was lots of hugging and kissing as they scored points, in an affectionate, encouraging sort of way. Commentators suggested the pair should 'get a room', forgetting they had an all-important final to win. Never has a pair looked so at ease with each other on court; the quick looks, the smiles, the high fives ... it was like a love story being played out. Who knew the ambience of Centre Court and the roaring, cheering crowd (who, let's face it, had slightly lost the etiquette of silence during rallies at this stage of the Championships) could produce such a match served in heaven? Not that this was going to be an easy match for the lovebirds;* they were facing the fifth seeds, Jonas Björkman and Alicia Molik, who had come from their semi-final match only four hours earlier after defeating Fabrice Santoro and Séverine Brémond.

Our pair (MuJan) didn't get off to the best start, going 2-0 down before fighting back thanks to some stinging cross-court forehands by Jelena and then Murray's stinging returns. Now the match was level at 3-3 and it became clear that Alicia was the weakest link of the opposition. Like a pair of smiling assassins, Jamie and Jelena felt that focusing their killer shots on her would be the key to securing this set. And so it was. When Jamie served at 5-4 for the first set, not even both players going for the ball at the same time (hey, it happens to the best of us) could stop them winning that set point. This was a final that showed the difference in the two pairs: the young, smiley and seemingly not fazed in the slightest by the occasion, compared to the older, slightly fazed by the occasion Jonas and Alicia, who were looking a little tired and fraught while the young 'uns were working so well together. There was trouble in paradise in the second set, however, when Jonas, now fully reconciled to working that bit more to cover for a weaker Alicia, brought his stinging backhand to the court and forced MuJan into playing catch-up for the whole of the second set, to no avail.

The action went to a third set and the spectators made the most of this Centre Court encore. Not even the security team surrounding three Swedish guys holding a flag could put a damper on the excitement of the final set, not to mention this enduring 'will they/won't they seal the deal' storyline (you can infer from this whatever you like, but I simply mean hold the trophy aloft).

The third set got off to a good start when Jamie showed the power of his serve, targeting Jonas's forehand as well as peppering body shots at Alicia. MuJan took the first game and then broke to go 2-0. It looked like they would face a break in the next game, when Alicia suddenly burst into life and battered over some much-needed motoring forehands. Now she and Jonas had three break points and the chance to get back into the third set, but the mighty MuJan saved them all. They were 3-0 ahead and could smell victory.

When it was Jelena's turn to serve, she was doing so for the match at 5-1. And in true final spirit, the crowd made sure they cheered every point won. Jelena served three winners (we did mention she was a fairly handy singles player) and Jamie volleyed home the winning shot. The couple who two weeks ago weren't even acquainted were the new Wimbledon champions. The pair were delighted, the crowd ecstatic, and little brother Andy, rising to his feet in the players' box, was clapping wholeheartedly. As with any Wimbledon occasion where history buffs can bring forward names of yonder to add clout to victory, this was the first time since Jeremy Bates and Jo Durie won in 1987 that the Wimbledon crowd had celebrated a British win. But it was so much more than that. The pair showed that playing tennis was fun, it was cheeky, it was relaxed and it was enjoyable. Of course, it's hard work, but watching these two in action, you would think all that was required was a positive attitude and a smile on your face.

*This was heavily speculated in the press and media at the time, but no romance blossomed for the pair. Jelena had a long-term boyfriend back in Serbia and, years later, confessed that she had some tricky conversations with him about the tabloid coverage on her homecoming.

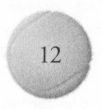

12

Pete Sampras vs Pat Rafter

Date: 9 July 2000
Score: 6-7, 7-6, 6-4, 6-2

'Whatever happened in my career or my
tennis or mentally, it happened for a reason.
In a lot of ways, I felt like I was born to win
Wimbledon.' Pete Sampras

WHEN THE daylight fades, the play stops. Well, that's what is supposed to happen. In the case of the 2000 Men's Singles final, the evening light was dimming across the spectators and it was only the action on court that provided the illumination. And that was the light at the end of the tunnel for six-time Wimbledon champion Pete Sampras as he sought a record seventh title. Sampras was the kind of athlete who was very much a loner but not alone. He was aloof but not rude, private but not disrespectful. Part of his 'champion quality' was, many speculated, his ability to focus on the game, not show emotion. He was also the sort of player that gave a tremendous impression that he was able, at any given point in a game, to shift up a gear, like a predator biding his time before deciding he's ready to inflict the fatal blow.

Sampras was on course to win his 13th Grand Slam that year at Wimbledon and had a serve that was often the fatal blow for many opponents. Even his second serves were unbelievable and, quite often, unreturnable. And yet this year felt different. He was carrying an injury that wasn't publicly acknowledged by his camp as Sampras didn't want to dwell on it (his practice before the final lasted just 15 minutes before he called it a day). And besides, his parents were flying in from California to watch the match, having never witnessed their son win a Grand Slam title. His parents were as private as their son; they didn't want to be seated in the players' box or draw any unnecessary attention to themselves, and it was only those in the Sampras camp that knew they were there.

After an hour's rain delay before anyone could even take a serve, the match started badly for the six-time champion. He knew his opponent, Australian Pat Rafter, had come through a tougher route to the final than him, beating No. 2 seed Andre Agassi in the semi-final, and would therefore be feeling, if not invincible, certainly quietly confident.

Midway through the first set, the dark clouds of doom (too dramatic?) surged forth over Centre Court and a 24-minute stoppage was announced. Then the players were only back on court for eight minutes before the spiteful rain came down again, and this time the players found themselves with two and a half hours of solitude. When play resumed, Sampras showed a more vulnerable side to his game. He double-faulted in the first-set tie-break, which Rafter won 12-10. Rafter then broke Sampras in the second set, gaining a strong 4-1 lead.

Sampras was making the sort of mistakes the Centre Court crowd had rarely seen from him before. When he hit one of his routine forehand drives too long, his shoulders slumped in an even rarer display of emotion while Rafter soaked in all the applause. Whether overconfidence or butterflies attacked Rafter's serve after that, we'll never know, but after a surprising double fault he started to look rattled. Sampras made his move. Failing to convert that lead in the second set frustrated Rafter further and Sampras was able to level the match and shift the dynamic of the game. Having won the previous six out of seven points in that second-set tie-break, the emotional aspect of the game shifted too. In just four or five minutes of play, Sampras had gone from losing to levelling the match – that shift was the boost he needed.

With the light beginning to look suspect, Sampras took the third set after moving in front early on in a tense fifth game that saw him break Rafter's serve for the first time after Rafter hit a volley into the net. The reactions from both players were becoming the talking point; with a clenched fist and glare over the net Sampras was focused, while Rafter was bouncing his racket on the ground in frustration.

The light continued to fade. At 8.11pm the crowds knew there was probably an hour's play left on court and no one wanted to leave without witnessing the crowning of a champion. And it looked like Sampras was going to take responsibility for getting the job done. Now with two sets under his belt, he was carried by momentum in the fourth set and very quickly secured a 5-2 advantage. He was going to be serving for the Championship and there were probably only about five minutes of light remaining on Centre Court for him to do it. He served out the match in style (and near darkness) and then, in a rare display of emotion (perhaps he was hoping the dim light would help hide his tears of joy), he searched the crowd for his parents. 'Where are my parents?' he mouthed to his coach in the players' box. After a quick point and wave indicating their general direction in the crowd, Sampras, overcome with emotion and only wanting to share that with two people, started climbing up through the spectators to hug his dad and mum. Slaps on the back, roaring applause and overwhelming cheers of celebration greeted the champion as he finally got to hug his parents, who were equally overcome with emotion. It was 8.57pm and that was the last time Sampras would hold the Wimbledon trophy aloft, in a magical dusky

Centre Court setting with the support of his parents and the love of a Wimbledon crowd. There is probably no better way to end.

13

Serena Williams and Venus Williams vs Julie Halard-Decugis and Ai Sugiyama

Date: 10 July 2000
Score: 6-3, 6-2

'It's our ambition to just take over tennis.'
Serena Williams

FRESH FROM lifting the aptly named Venus Rosewater Dish, Venus Williams was on a high from her victory in the Ladies' Singles final but wanted more silverware to add to her trophy cabinet. And who better to join forces with than her younger sister, Serena, whom she had defeated in the semis?

Wimbledon was only the third time the sisters had played in a match as a doubles team and so they were wild-card entries. They had a fairly seamless start to the tournament, winning in straight sets against their opponents in their early-stage matches. But the test came when they went up against Martina Navratilova and her partner, Mariaan de Swardt, in the quarter-final. They lost the first set (whaat??) but came back to seal victory with wins in the next two sets.

The Centre Court crowd were lively that afternoon. These weren't the packed crowds either Williams sister was used to having cheering them on, but it was near capacity and those watching were part of history – if Serena and Venus won they would be the first siblings to win the Ladies' Doubles, and if Ai Sugiyama was victorious with her partner, Julie Halard-Decugis, she would be the first Japanese woman to win a title since 1975.

The powerful might of the Williams sisters prevailed. In just over one hour and ten minutes, they did what they had set out to do and lifted the Doubles trophy. After winning the toss but losing the first game on Venus's serve, the match didn't get off to the best start. But the sheer power play and force behind the returns, not to mention some double faults by the French-Japanese pair, gave the sisters room to break back. Doubles is always a spectacle of rallies and expertise, but the crowd whooping and cheering as each shot is returned forms part of the unrivalled joy of watching Singles stars join forces. The shouts of 'C'mon, sisters!' echoed around the court, and even when they clanked rackets for the winning set point, it didn't matter.

Serena and Venus took the first set 6-3 and then broke Ai's serve in the first game of the second set. It wasn't that their opponents didn't put up a fight (although on paper it does look that way); it was more that the luck and the power were in the Williams sisters' court, and when you are playing with your sibling there is an easy chemistry that some unrelated players find hard to match in years of playing together. With Ladies' champion Venus sending 90mph first serves, it wasn't long before they went 2-0 up and then broke again for 3-0. Things got a bit lax (we jest) on Serena's serve to allow Ai and Julie to win their fourth point of the entire second set. It must have been the momentum they needed (we jest again) as Julie managed to win her service game to end their losing run of eight games. Ai managed to hold her serve too (after Venus served for the sixth and won), giving the pair a semi-respectable two games to five. But it just wasn't ever going to be enough. Now Serena was serving for her and her sister to win the Doubles title and, on Championship point, served an ace. That, folks, is how you do it.

This was the first time that two sisters had won the Ladies' Doubles title; the fact they had done it as wild cards showed what a formidable team they were. And the fact that they had done it on little sleep, having been out at the Champions Ball until 2am the night before (they had to play on Monday because rain had delayed the Men's final on Sunday), was just pure class. The fact that they then went on to win the Ladies' Doubles in 2002, and then again in 2008, 2009, 2012 and 2016, shows how powerful sisterhood really is.

14

Boris Becker vs Kevin Curren

Date: 7 July 1985
Score: 6-3, 6-7, 7-6, 6-4

'I love the winning, I can take the losing, but most of all I love to play.' Boris Becker

WHEN PLAYERS enter the Championships unseeded, there is always an air of expectation about them, a sense of suspense as their possibility is revealed. When Boris Becker entered Wimbledon as a 17-year-old unseeded German, only one man suggested he would go the distance – Johan Kriek, the South African player Becker had beaten in the final at Queen's Club a week before the Championships started. 'If he plays like that, he'll win Wimbledon,' he stated.

But few paid attention. McEnroe was the reigning champion and No. 1 seed, while Jimmy Connors, Pat Cash and Kevin Curren were all in the top eight and hoping for glory. As the competition progressed, it was Curren who quickly became the favourite after he spectacularly wiped out McEnroe in the quarter-final and then Connors in the semi without dropping a set. Meanwhile the young German player who nobody had been paying particular attention to had been steadily making his way through the rounds. But when Becker made it into the last 16 and then the quarter-final and then the semi-final, Wimbledon finally started to pay attention. Becker's win against Anders Järryd (2-6, 7-6, 6-3, 6-3 in the semi-final) was phenomenal, but what was more impressive was that this young player didn't seem fazed in the slightest.

Not that his fellow finalist, Curren, seemed fazed by the prospect of playing an unseeded nobody. In fact, he was so at ease that the night before the final, secure in the knowledge that he was firing on all cylinders, his huge serve was doing what it should and that the teenager would most probably be the one to crack under the immense pressure, Curren went to a Bruce Springsteen concert. 'It was phenomenal,' he later conceded. 'It wasn't really like me because I wasn't a big concert-goer, but he was the man right then.'

As the morning of the final dawned and the spectators started filing into their seats, everyone was feeling a little nervous for the teenager. Commentators were eager to report that if Becker won he would be the youngest ever player in the history of the Championships to do so. And the first ever unseeded player. And the first German. But

Becker showed no such nerves and sauntered onto court next to Curren looking relaxed and instantly at ease in his surroundings – although he made sure he was first to his lucky Centre Court chair.

If there was ever a player that looked instantly at home in such grand surroundings with the world watching, not to mention thousands of pairs of eyes all boring into you at once, Becker was the master. He didn't show fear because he had none; this was another match to him. As the sun shone down, Becker made the first move, breaking Curren the first time he served and winning the first set without much of a struggle after that.

The explosive serves that Wimbledon had seen in the McEnroe and Connors matches were long gone and, unbelievably, it was the more experienced Curren who was struggling to find his rhythm. Up against a fearless teenager and with the second set going to a tie-break, the older player managed to hang on.

The match wasn't so much a lesson in youthful enthusiasm, it was more that Becker seemed to possess the athleticism, the power and the unwavering belief to chase down every ball, tumbling and diving at every turn, in a display of hearty hunger. Curren had the chance to show the youngster what for when he broke Becker early in the third set, and perhaps a glimmer of hope started to dawn that the German might now be buckling under pressure. Becker's formerly white top and shorts were now covered in dust from throwing himself at Curren's unreturnable serves, and he started to let out the odd shout of annoyance as Curren won points from him. But rather than buckle, the teenager used his annoyance as ammo and lifted his game to win the third set. When he broke Curren in the fourth with a series of tremendously forceful returns, he went on to hold his service game with three thundering aces and soon found himself serving for the Championship at 5-4.

Becker knew his bullet serves were all that was standing between him and the title, but suddenly the nerves did seem to catch up with him. He started with a double fault before winning the next three points to go 40-15. Standing in front of two Championship points, he faltered again, double-faulting. Now there was only one Championship point. The frustrated cry from Becker matched the cheers and shouts from the crowd. 'I just started looking up and praying: "God, give me a first serve because I don't know what I'm going to do with that second serve."' And the serve did indeed come; an ace making Becker the new young champion. With his arms held in the air, head thrown back and roaring along with the crowd, Becker had done it. A new, strawberry-blond dawn was breaking.

15

Virginia Wade vs Betty Stöve

Date: 2 July 1977
Score: 4-6, 6-3, 6-1

*'I wanted to prove that I really deserved
to be out there among the champions.'*
Virginia Wade

THE SETTING could not have been more idyllic. This
was the centenary year of Wimbledon, as well as the
Queen's Silver Jubilee. Surely the cream on top of the
strawberries wasn't going to be a British winner as well,
was it? Of course, you know your history, you know there
is a happy ending to this specific tale, which meant that
it was a truly momentous and patriotic occasion. Never
before had there been such a rousing version of 'Land of
Hope and Glory' sung by the spectators caught up by the
occasion. Never had the cheers been so deafening from the
14,000-strong crowd. Never had Centre Court produced
such patriotic fervour that, even though Virginia Wade
lost the first set, everyone held on to the firm belief that

the No. 3 seed and British darling would still win. Never before had ball girls taken part in the Championships either. It was a tournament year full of firsts.

This was Virginia's 16th attempt at the Wimbledon Ladies' Singles title. She was nine days away from her 32nd birthday and she had something to prove. Her fans showed unwavering loyalty and she wanted to repay them. She didn't want to be known as the player who wasn't champion material; she wanted to prove once and for all that she had what it took to lift that trophy high above her head and declare to the tennis elite, the commentators, the world, that she could do it.

In terms of the standard of tennis on display, this was no high-quality contest. Virginia had displayed some of the best tennis of her life in her previous match of the Championships, the semi-final against the reigning champion, Chris Evert, who she beat 6-2, 4-6, 6-1. Chris had only lost two out of her 56 singles matches that year and had underestimated the power of Wimbledon's heroine as a stunned Centre Court crowd watched on. Virginia had beaten the reigning champion. According to one newspaper, if you had put a bet on her reaching the final to play Betty Stöve, you would have received odds of around 1000-1. So this final was more a game of emotion, of double faults, of edginess and British perseverance. But it didn't matter. As Virginia and her Dutch opponent, Betty Stöve, came out onto Centre Court that Friday in early July, the crowd were in full 'Last Night Of The Proms' mode. Watching them turn and curtsy were not only the Queen and the Duke of Edinburgh on their first visit to the All England Club since 1962 (which was also the year Virginia made her first of 16 consecutive appearances), but tennis royalty as well. Seated behind the Queen were four of the most recent British title holders, including Kitty Godfree (1924, 1926), Dorothy Round (1934, 1937), Angela Mortimer (1961) and Ann Jones (1969).

It was an occasion that could have easily crushed a mere mortal. But Virginia had decided long before the gates opened at SW19 that this was her year. 'I think knowing that the Queen was going to be there made me feel, "Well, if she is going to be there, I'd better be there. And if I am there, I better win."' With the expectation of a cheering crowd, the long wait to prove you can be champion and the Jubilee year all weighing on your shoulders, there might have been one or two fans who would have excused Virginia in the days following had she succumbed to the pressure of the occasion. Even with a good-luck note from Arthur Ashe, an American player who shared the same birthday as Virginia, which advised her to 'camp out at the net', the match didn't get off to the best of starts when the British star repeatedly failed to take advantage of Betty's double faults. Betty was one of the tallest WTA players of her time, while Virginia had a smooth delivery and arguably one of the best serves in the women's game on her side.

When she lost the first set, it was now or never to prove that she had the guts to carry on. The enthusiastic crowd knew she was capable of it, but did she? It was in the middle of the second set that the tide began to turn. The lack of jaw-dropping rallies meant that many of the points were won on the serve. With Betty showcasing nine double faults and rarely able to employ her infamous serve-and-volley winners, Virginia took advantage and stole a 3-0 lead in the second set. But if Virginia had royalty and the patriotic crowd on her side, Betty's family were out in force in the players' box, and their rallying cries helped Betty mount an attack to draw the set level at 3-3.

Now it was Virginia's turn to show she could hold steady. And she did, driving home four first serves to win the seventh game and then taking advantage of more double faults from Betty, earning herself the chance to serve for the second set. And she took it. Now the crowd really had something to cheer about. The momentum had swung back to the home opponent, and now she just needed to hold her nerve ...

And she did. The final set lasted just 26 minutes. It would have been shorter had Betty not mounted a valiant last-ditch attempt to win the fifth game in which she was 0-40 down. But the crowd, the press box and the

British public were given the victory they had longed for; Wimbledon had a new champion and she was one of ours.

The noise level from the crowd didn't abate until long after the match was over; even the Queen was inaudible as she presented the trophy to the new champion. 'At the end I couldn't hear what the Queen was saying to me,' confessed Virginia. 'But it was just great to see her lips moving.'

16

Fred Perry vs Donald Budge

Date: 2 July 1936
Score: 5-7, 6-4, 6-3, 6-4

*'I didn't aspire to be a good sport;
"Champion" was good enough for me.'*
Fred Perry

'THE WAIT is finally over' is an oft-heard phrase from the press box at SW19, but you can bet your last punnet of 'berries that it was definitely used in reference to a player about to achieve the status of one of the greatest unsung heroes of his time – Fred Perry. Until Andy Murray clinched the Men's Wimbledon Singles title in 2013 (see Match 35), the name Fred Perry was thrown around each year another British player tried and failed to secure a Wimbledon title. But back in the day, the first triple Men's Singles winner wasn't celebrated from baseline to net, as is the way these days. In fact, as one journalist remarked, when he first lifted the Wimbledon trophy aloft in 1934 there was 'a strange lack of excitement' among the crowd of spectators.

Fred was, in that era, not one to play by the rules of British society. Unlike other players who behaved with decorum and gentlemanly manners, Fred was ruthless on the court and refused to conceal an ambitious streak that other players deemed ungentlemanly and offensive. His attitude to wanting to win stood in stark contrast to the good-mannered and noble ethos of the All England Club, and it was after his Wimbledon win in 1934 that he left the country to join a small professional travelling circuit in America. But back to his last win at the All England Club and the game before the big final.

Fred was facing one of his most serious threats in that year's Championships in the form of Donald Budge, who hadn't quite hit top form but was fast becoming one of the top contenders in the sport. Would Perry be able to defend his title against the American? Well, yes, but it took every ounce of greatness to do so. Perhaps on paper it looks like the first set was the sole twitchy round, but that would do both players a disservice. They had played each other twice before, once in the Davis Cup and once in California, and on both occasions Fred had secured a convincing victory. But on Centre Court today, with the bright sun shining a spotlight on the sport's biggest stage, the two-time successive champion was facing a tricky first set.

In a time when a serve was seen more of the start of a rally rather than a big power-play point, Perry went up

5-3 in the first set, but then it looked like he was getting ahead of himself in his eagerness to get a set under his belt. He was within one point of the set three times, but wasn't able to secure it. When he drove a forehand into the net, the set was tied at 5-5. Budge had turned the tables and used the change in fortune to drum home a break of serve and then hold his own to take the first set from the defending champion. Perry's fire was ignited, his concentration sharpened. In that second set you could almost feel the glow emitting from a man who was firing on all cylinders and hitting perfectly executed shots.

When he went 4-1 up in the second set, and then 0-40 on Budge's serve, the champion looked to have returned in all his glory. But Budge wasn't 'budging' and, in an almighty display of resolve that saw the crowd respond with rousing and lengthy applause, he brought the second set back level at 4-4. He was in no yielding mood, proving that whatever shot the champion sent over would be fired back in equal measure.

The challenger was not ready to give in. And yet, even with a more polished forehand and steadier lobs, perhaps the occasion or the thousands of pairs of eyes watching him were too much and his attack lost some of its venom. When he pummelled a smash into the net and served two double faults in the ninth game, Perry broke. And then he took the second set, losing only one point in his service game (his own double fault).

Perry went on to secure the third set, allowing Budge to hold his serve on just three occasions, but by the fourth set Budge was back to his charging form and took the lead 4-2. It was a somewhat menacing attack and it took every ounce of Perry's unflinching resolve to remain calm whilst he produced some of the match's most breathtaking deadly volleys. His running forehand drives would not have found the precision landing ground they did if a mere mortal had played them, yet Perry was now playing in a league of his own and they were played to perfection. He lost only three more points and, as the American netted his final shot, Perry jumped over the net to shake the hand of his valiant yet defeated opponent. The crowds knew their home champion had battled hard and had proved that he wasn't going to give up his Wimbledon crown easily.

When he played Baron von Cramm in the final, it was, without exaggeration, a walk in the park. Perry lifted the Wimbledon crown after just 45 minutes of play, winning 6-1, 6-1, 6-0 over his German opponent. He didn't need to prove himself; he had been there, done that, got the T-shirt and shown that he had the hunger of a champion in the semis. Little did he know how agonisingly long it would be until any British player got close to holding that trophy aloft again.

17

Martina Hingis vs Jana Novotná

Date: 5 July 1997
Score: 2-6, 6-3, 6-3

'I told her I'm getting a little old now ...'
Jana Novotná

AT 16 years and 278 days old, Martina Hingis was the youngest female player to win the Ladies' Singles title since Lottie Dodd in 1887. Absent because of injury, Steffi Graf saw her No. 1 seeding go to young Martina, who won her first Grand Slam title at the Australian Open. Steffi was the two-time Wimbledon defending champion, but she was unable to play as Martina took the Championships by storm. The crowds at Wimbledon had a soft spot for Jana, though. She had been inconsolable after the 1993 final when she went up against Steffi Graf and looked likely to become the new champion. But then there was an epic third-set collapse, and the image of Jana crying on the Duchess of Kent's shoulder at the trophy presentation remains a more memorable image than Steffi's victory. Jana was the bridesmaid but never (not yet, anyway) the bride, and so it was again four years later. This was her 42nd Grand Slam singles tournament, while Martina was still new to this main stage, playing in only her third major final in 11 events. It was no secret that this youngster, named after tennis legend Martina Navratilova, would cause an upset in the tournament, but could she go the distance at the All England Club?

Martina, dubbed the 'Swiss Miss' by the media, was full of excitement as she walked out with Jana to a standing ovation from the crowd. She would give all the spectators a slice of history if she won the match, but would that pressure help or hinder her game?

Jana had a smooth all-court game, while Martina, not known for her power, could dominate with a diverse range of shots. It was the bridesmaid who seemed to be showing off her prowess in the first set, making sure she dominated her young opponent by executing a range of attacking shots that left Martina unable to make her mark on the first set. She lost 6-2.

Now, as any teenager knows, when you are faced with not getting your own way, a strange surge of energy and focus develops. It was in the second set that the crowds realised the 16-year-old Swiss was not going to bow down easily. A frustrated bounce of her racket on the grass as she took her seat showed her frustration. Martina had youthful arrogance on her side; she was now an angry teenager with a point to prove. If the side smirk was to show anything, it was that she was in charge.

And she was. In the second set she took advantage of her first break against Jana and took a 2-0 lead. She took the second set in much the same way Jana had taken the first, with a 6-3 win. They were equal now, just as the sun burst through to shine brightly on Centre Court, casting a spotlight on the remainder of the match as the deciding final set began.

After a few looks of outright astonishment from Martina at a couple of missed shots, she started to find her rhythm and Jana was under pressure. When Jana was serving to stay in the match at 3-5, there was a sense that things were going to end very quickly unless she could produce the sort of tennis that would stop Martina in her tracks. She started with a double fault (0-15) before Martina sent a lob flying off court (15-15). One of the best rallies of the match followed, but ended with Martina hitting another long shot (30-15). But then Jana made a silly error (30-30) and was now just two points from another heartbreaking defeat. Martina seized her chance, pulling out a terrific backhand shot under pressure (30-40). One point away from losing again, Jana didn't crumble (well, not on her second serve) and brought the game to deuce. Jana played a superb angled volley to take the advantage, but it wasn't enough. After playing a long shot to go back to deuce, Martina took the advantage with another accurate passing shot and now a second Championship point was in her grasp. She wasn't going to let it go for a second time, leaping up in the air with her hands high when she played the winning shot. 'Yes!' she cried, running to the net as the new Wimbledon Ladies' champion.

It was pure uninhibited joy from Martina. She was the youngest female player to win Wimbledon this century. Suddenly, you didn't see a professional, cool tennis player on court, just an overexcited, giddy teenager whose dream of winning a second Grand Slam title had come true. She threw her racket into the crowd and no one could wipe the smile from her face as she lapped up the deserved applause. The Duchess of Kent was again on hand to comfort Jana, who wasn't as emotional this time, but felt equally as desolate at getting so close yet so far once again. 'I told her I'm getting a little old now and she said to me my third time would be lucky,' revealed Jana, years later.

Martina went on to win the US Open, beating up-and-coming Venus Williams, but lost out to Iva Majoli in the French Open, thus denying her a clean sweep of Grand Slams.

And what of our bridesmaid? With the words of the Duchess of Kent ringing in her ears – 'One day you will do it, I know you will!' – Jana's dreams finally came true the following year as she held aloft the Venus Rosewater Dish. She was the oldest first-time champion in the Open Era, but it didn't matter, she had done it. If there was anyone who could show what perseverance, determination and pure strength of character looked like, Jana was it. And let it be said, 'No-No' Novotná never gave up.

18

Nicolas Mahut and Pierre-Hugues Herbert vs Julien Benneteau and Édouard Roger-Vasselin

Date: 9 July 2016
Score: 6-4, 7-6, 6-3

*'Now I can come into the press conference
as a Wimbledon champion. It's great.'*
Nicolas Mahut

THIS MATCH made history by being the first all-French final at the All England Club. Mahut and Herbert were the top seeds and had won the US Open title the previous year, so when they faced their fellow countrymen on Centre Court in the final, there was a whiff of expectation about them.

And there was a chance for Mahut to make yet more history, having previously entered Wimbledon's record books for taking part in the longest tennis match of all time when he lost to John Isner in 2010 after an epic battle that lasted 11 hours and five minutes (for more on that three-day event, see Match 47).

Thanks to the rain-interrupted first week of the tournament, there was a bit of an upset to the doubles camp when officials announced that they would be reducing the format of the Men's Doubles from best-of-five sets, as with the Men's Singles, to best-of-three. This new ruling was originally introduced for the first round of play only, but the continuing inclement weather saw them extend this new format into the second-round matches, prompting some of the big names of the doubles game to voice their concerns. American Scott Lipsky took to social media, accusing Wimbledon bosses of panicking after one day of rain and stating that this was a 'bad move'. There was definitely an air of imbalance when it came to scheduling the doubles matches. For only the fourth time in the tournament's history, the first Sunday, normally an idle day, saw two first-round Men's Doubles matches being played while six teams were already in the third round and all other teams in the second. Sam Groth, along with his partner Robert Lindstedt, also believed changing the format was bad for the game, stating that doubles needs the extra two sets as a way of ensuring the best duo wins. Wimbledon was one of the few tournaments that used five sets for the Men's Doubles, while other Grand Slam events played the entire tournament as a best-of-three. Mahut, however, didn't think the reduction in sets in the early rounds was a problem. Before he started his doubles campaign with his partner, Herbert, he faced him in the third round of the Singles competition, winning 7-6, 6-4, 3-6, 6-3. But the fourth round was as far as his Singles journey went, when he lost in straight sets to Sam Querrey.

So the two Frenchmen were now firmly focused on the Doubles. Both teams for this match had a few hiccups en route to Centre Court. For Mahut and Herbert, these didn't come until the semi-final when, for the first time in the tournament, they had to contest all five sets. They faced Max Mirnyi and Treat Huey and, after winning the first set quite comfortably, lost the next two. After battling back in the fourth, they claimed the deciding fifth set and Mahut was one step closer to lifting a piece of Wimbledon silverware. Benneteau and Vasselin struggled long before they reached the semis, needing all five sets to secure a win in the third round, then again in the fourth, before facing Jamie Murray and Bruno Soares in the quarter-final. The crowd were behind the No. 3 seeds, but the Frenchmen took the opening two sets, before losing the next two and going all out in the final set to win 6-4, 6-4, 6-7, 6-7, 10-8.

So to the final we go, and if the Centre Court crowd had come in prepared for the long haul (Mahut still carried his 'marathon man' nickname with him – and likely always will – whenever he stepped onto a grass court), they might have been disappointed. No epic three-day action here (see Match 47); just an athletic, almost gymnastic display by both French duos that was over in two hours and six minutes.

The play was quick and reactive, the precision of the shots magical, and the action at the net immediate as all players sought those small spaces on court that weren't covered by a long-reaching Frenchman. And there was a real sense of camaraderie about the game – Mahut and Benneteau knew each other well as they had played and won seven junior doubles titles as teenagers in 1999, and all four players knew they were making history by playing in the final. For one pair, sadly, that had to be enough. Herbert liked to mix his serves to keep his opponent guessing and, with a mixture of slices, spins and flat first serves, he did just that. He found a form of aggression with Mahut that saw him shoot down a lot of net play. Meanwhile Vasselin, widely regarded as the best returner in the game, justified that label with his unnaturally quick reactions. The crowd were treated to a fabulous French final from both duos, with Mahut and Herbert falling to their knees to embrace as the winning shot was played. Bien joué, lads, bien joué.

19

Ricardo Pancho Gonzales vs Charlie Pasarell

Date: 26 June 1969
Score: 22-24, 1-6, 16-14, 6-3, 11-9

*'I walked off the court and I was distraught.
I could not believe I lost that match. I then
felt a big Wimbledon towel draped over my
head. It was Pancho, he put an arm around
my shoulders and said, "Kid, I got lucky."'*
Charlie Pasarell

AS FIRST-ROUND matches go, you would be hard pushed to find one that deserves a place on this list more than this emotionally draining battle between a man described as an 'ageing lion' and his young former protégé. At 41 years old, Ricardo Pancho 'The Big Cheese' Gonzales had been on the cusp of greatness for the past 15 years and was considered one of the best in the 50s era – he was World No. 1 for eight years. In contrast, Charlie Pasarell was 25 years old, beginning to make his mark in the new Open Era of tennis and his future looked bright. The two men were no strangers; Pasarell had been coached by Gonzales, who knew where his strengths and weaknesses were on court, having trained and practised with him in America.

As the two men came onto Centre Court, no one could have foreseen the impact the match would have on this year's tournament, let alone on the way tie-break sets would later be capped (more on that later). They began playing at 7pm on a cool, cloudy Tuesday. What happened on court that evening, and the following day, made Wimbledon history. If any of the spectators thought that the older, greyer opponent might yield fairly quickly to his younger opponent as the match progressed, they could not have been more wrong.

Play was even in the first set, the players matching each other in the power and perfect execution of their shots. Both players held serve in the first 45 games (yes, 45), with Gonzales able to save set point 11 times in 18 games. And the games kept totting up. At last, it was Pasarell who managed to convert the 12th set point, breaking serve with a beautifully executed lob that just caught the baseline. He had been playing to what he perceived as Gonzales's weakness, keeping the ball low, chipping shots over the net and following these up with overhead lobs, in the belief that the older player would tire. Gonzales liked to get into the net quickly and tightly, so being forced to bend low by Pasarell's tactical play was, as expected, exhausting.

With the light fading on Centre Court, Gonzales was keen to call it a day and asked the umpire, Mike Gibson, to suspend play until the next day. But Gibson didn't think there was a problem with the light and refused his request, sparking an angry and exhausted Gonzales to rant on court. 'How the hell can I play when I can't see?' fumed The Big Cheese, clearly fatigued and frustrated.

'Play on,' came the unruffled response from Gibson, sparking a further outburst from Gonzales, who was refusing to let this argument die. As the Centre Court crowd started to boo this unsportsmanlike outburst, they only added fuel to the fire. Gonzales threw his racket to the ground. He continued to argue that he couldn't see the ball and the boos continued to increase in volume. But Gibson would not be moved, the second set was on. Taking advantage of his mentor's state of annoyance, not to mention weariness, Pasarell took the second set with a straightforward 6-1 after just 18 minutes of play. As Gibson finally announced that play was suspended, Gonzales was still fuming.

'He slammed down his rackets, throwing some into the net, and stormed off court,' remembered Pasarell. 'He was so angry. I went to the net and gathered up his stuff, asking one of the ball boys to help me return them to the locker room.'

The players had been out on court for two hours and 20 minutes and the consensus was that Gonzales was going to have an epic battle on his hands to come back from two sets down if he wanted to continue his journey in the Championships. What no one realised was that the old lion still had a lot of fight left in him.

The following day, just before 2pm, the sun shone down on Centre Court as the players came back out to continue their match. Most assumed that Pasarell, considered to be the best first-round player in the tournament and only needing one more set to claim victory, would seal the deal. It's worth noting at this point that there were no chairs for the players to sit down on between games. They were not introduced until 1975.

The third set signified a new start and Gonzales came out fresh and ready for action, the anger from the previous night forgotten. He knew he had unfinished business and the formidable giant was ready to go. The first half of the set didn't start well. Pasarell was piling on the pressure and Gonzales's formidable serve was shortening. But instead of his tactile play of wearing down Gonzales with chips and lobs, a combination that had worked so well previously, Pasarell played more standard forehands that lacked either power or attack. He was nervous, and he missed two crucial chances to break serve when the games were tied at 8-8 and then 10-10. The youngster was losing confidence. At 14-15 he served two appalling double faults and sprayed a backhand well wide to give Gonzales the third set. This was always going to be the danger for Pasarell. Gonzales knew where his weaknesses lay; he had coached him through a lot of them and was now using them against him.

The fourth set began with both players eager to forget any mistakes of the previous 30-game third set and start afresh, but in the seventh game disaster loomed for Pasarell, with Gonzales taking control of a rally with a rhythmical display of angled shots, and his young opponent went on to lose the set with a double fault.

The fifth set became a display of unparalleled sportsmanship and showed both men – differing in age, attacking style and attitude – become focused to the point of solitude. The Centre Court crowd might as well not have been there; this was about two men and their stamina and endurance. With new fight in his racket (even though two of the strings from his favourite rackets had broken), Pasarell decided to reassess his tactics again. 'I knew I had to move him around because I thought he'd be stiff,' revealed Pasarell. 'But he won the third and fourth sets and I now decided to go for a few shots.'

If the afternoon had been an unforgettable one up to that point, the fifth set would round it off as one of the greatest opening games in the history of the Championships. Pasarell had seven match points in the final set, twice when Gonzales was serving at love-40.

One of these occasions, when all the glory might have gone to Pasarell, served up one of the most memorable points of the match. Gonzales rarely missed his first serve, but when he did – and with Pasarell on match point on the second serve – Pasarell decided to go for a backhand return to Gonzales's backhand side that left Gonzales diving at full stretch and falling onto the court with his racket thrown from his hand. But not before he had connected with the shot, which barely crept over the net but had such backspin that it span back into the net.

By this point Gonzales was trying to conserve all his energy, regularly leaning on his racket between points and trying to control the game by exerting as little energy as physically possible. He was crippled with cramp, but his mind was sharp. He was a ferocious opponent and this old dog was adamant he hadn't had his day. When Pasarell overhit a lob on his seventh match point at 8-7, Gonzales took control of the fight. He won the last 11 points of the match, bringing this long tale to an end and completing one of the most emotionally charged endurance victories ever witnessed at Wimbledon. In total, 112 games had been played over a total of five hours and 20 minutes. It was a record-breaking match in every sense.

As one newspaper reporter noted, 'The road back was a long one and Gonzales, a hero in every step, made it. This restless, fidgety giant dominates the court and would not lie down.'

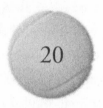

20

Margaret Court vs Billie Jean King

Date: 3 July 1970
Score: 14-12, 11-9

*'Pressure is a privilege, it only comes to those
who earn it.'* Billie Jean King

TWO YEARS prior to this epic match (which can only be described as a world-class display of tennis), Wimbledon turned professional. The tournament began its first 'Open Era' and became the second Grand Slam tournament to offer prize money and allow professionals and amateurs to enter. The winner of the Men's Singles title would receive £2,000, while the winner of the Ladies' Singles would receive £750. The winner in that first Open Era was Billie Jean King, who was also the first ever champion to use a metal racket – a racket that was heavily examined by Princess Marina, who presented Billie with the trophy in 1968. Now fast forward two years and Billie was back in the final, this time facing Australian Margaret Court, an old rival. Back in 1962

Billie had caused an upset when, at just 18 years old and playing in only her second ever Wimbledon match, she beat Margaret – who was the top seed – 1-6, 6-3, 7-5 in the opening match of the tournament. The rivalry was fierce. Billie had lost out to Ann Jones the previous year and was gunning to regain her status as Wimbledon Queen. Ann had not returned to defend her title and Billie was looking for a fourth win at the All England Club. Margaret, who had briefly retired in 1966, had come back and won three out of four Grand Slam singles titles the previous year. This year she wanted to get all four and made a good start when she beat Kerry Melville Reid in the Australian Open and then Helga Niessen Masthoff in the French Open final. And now Billie at Wimbledon was standing in her way.

It was the first time the Championships had been broadcast in colour, another move that underlined the changing times of the sport. So it was fitting that this match was about to showcase some of the most breathtaking and thrilling tennis ever witnessed in a final. It is often widely agreed that final matches do not always showcase the best tennis, due perhaps to the sense of occasion adding pressure on the players and causing relatively unremarkable games. Not this match. Playing as if their lives depended on every point, Billie and Margaret were going head-to-head in a battle of wills and resilience. What made their utter determination and gritty resolve all the more remarkable was that they were both struggling with injuries; Margaret had ankle issues that required an injection of painkillers, while Billie had a knee injury that would require surgery a few weeks after the tournament finished.

Not that you would have guessed it on that day. Playing in front of a packed Royal Box – including Prime Minister Edward Heath, Princess Margaret, Princess Alexandra and Princess Anne – Billie and Margaret were about to produce one of the most compelling contests the Championships had ever seen. This wasn't going to be a quick affair or a swift execution. Right from the first game, the crowd sensed a hard-fought battle lay ahead – here were two gloriously gifted and athletic players at the top of their game.

When Billie served at 5-4 for the first set, it looked like she would take an early lead. But each game had produced long rallies that showcased a range of shots, and this game was no different. Commentators were calling this tenth game of the set an important one for Margaret to win (which she did), little knowing they had a further 16 games to play. At 12 games all (the tie-break would not be introduced at Wimbledon until the following year) Margaret held her serve and then finally broke Billie's to win the first set. It was one of the longest first sets to be played by either sex in a Wimbledon singles final, at one hour and 30 minutes.

This was a masterclass in tennis from both players. Margaret's service and smash were flawless, her lobs, like Billie's, relentlessly accurate. If you were being picky, you might argue that Margaret was slightly tentative on the forehand drive and volley, while Billie showcased some cross-court backhands fit for a king. In the second set, Billie was feeling the pressure as she served to stay in the match at 6-7. She won, with Margaret failing to convert her first opportunity at a match point. At that point the referee had to tell the crowd to stay quiet during the rallies so as not to put off the players. Not that anyone could break the stride of these two.

Billie held her serve two more times to stay in the match. At nine games all, with Margaret serving, momentum swung in her favour when she went 40-0 up to a disgruntled Billie who had become frustrated by a line call. Once again Billie was serving to stay in the match. It was a game that saw her fight off five Championship points, but it was point number six that proved too much. She lost the final by driving a forehand into the net, a fairly sad and mundane finish to an otherwise outstanding match. The players came to the net to acknowledge each other's part in an epic battle, while the crowd were on their feet, acknowledging that they had witnessed a truly momentous final.

21

Todd Woodbridge and Mark Woodforde vs Sandon Stolle and Paul Haarhuis

Date: 8 July 2000
Score: 6-3, 6-4, 6-1

*'This was perfect, I was very pleased
that today, win or lose, we were going to
end our partnership out on that court.'*
Todd Woodbridge

WHEN YOU think of men's doubles and Wimbledon winners, you would be hard pressed to think of a doubles duo more formidable than the 'Woodies', the partnership of Australians Todd Woodbridge and Mark Woodforde. This was the year that they were on course for their sixth Wimbledon win, a record in the Open Era, yet first they had to take on the mighty Canadian duo of Daniel Nestor and Sébastien Lareau in the quarter-final. It took all their self-belief and focus to remain contenders in the Championships as an epic three-hour battle played out on Court 13. At two sets to one down, perhaps the realisation dawned that, for one of the Woodies at least, this would be the last shot at glory and the chance to win a record sixth title – Woodbridge would be back, but Woodforde was hanging up his racket. Something clicked and they managed to overcome their opponents to progress to the semi-final where, riding high from their previous match, they were unstoppable once again. The glory days were back, the boys still had it.

Since 1993 they had reigned supreme, winning the Championships for five consecutive years and now, after a break of three years, they were back for one final blast, one last hurrah. The match took place on Centre Court and the Aussie duo were welcomed onto the main stage like they were Wimbledon's own sweethearts. In a sense, having been part of the history of men's doubles for so long, they were. This was the Ant and Dec of the tennis world, the Morecambe and Wise, the Laurel and Hardy, the Two Ronnies … It had been almost a decade since the Woodies made their debut appearance at the All England Club, but their standard of play, drive and enthusiasm had withstood the test of time. Where Todd was able to anticipate play, Mark played imaginatively. Their 'I' formation allowed them to play to their strengths, and helped to create some indecision in their opponents. They brought their individual skills to a game where teamwork was needed, and did it in one fluid motion. Their opponents in the final, Sandon Stolle and Paul Haarhuis, were another Australian duo, but they had only been playing together for four months. This inexperience showed. Or maybe the ease between the Woodies highlighted any minor crack in an opposition's relationship – think of the loved-up Kylie and Jason relationship against the fractious Madge and Harold (that's showing our age). The top-seeded Woodies set up an impenetrable curtain at the net during the tougher rallies, portraying a sense of 'none shall pass'. The rhythm of a strong serve by one, a fierce volley to compensate for a solid return by the other, and then a smash by the server is the way they won most of their points and then the Championship on Centre Court that day.

The match-winning point was a masterclass in teamwork and effectiveness, crafted over 11 Grand Slam wins and a record-breaking 60 tournament victories. A looping lob from Mark followed by a feeble response gave Todd the chance to showcase his killer instincts with an unchallenged volley. As the crowd rose to their feet, the relief from the pair was clear. They hadn't publicly stated that going out on a win would be the best way to bid farewell to SW19, but they were going to do just that and they were elated. After seeing them settle back into action so swiftly and easily, many spectators and commentators queried why Mark would want to end this formidable partnership. Why would he break up the band, which still showed such strength and ability? But a line had to be drawn somewhere, and the chalky service line at the All England Club seemed perfect. Besides, at 34 years old, five years older than his partner, and with a wife expecting their first child in January, it was as good an excuse as any. With a wave to the crowd and an uncharacteristic hug for the referee, Alan Mills, this was indeed a memorable send-off.

They were to finish their partnership officially at the Olympic Games in Sydney later that year, where they took the silver medal. The following year, a solitary Woody returned to SW19 with a new partner, Sweden's Jonas Björkman. Woodbridge and Björkman (Woodman? Bridgork? We'll work on that one.) went on to win the Men's Doubles title for three years running from 2002, before Todd retired with a record-breaking 83 men's doubles titles.

22

Steffi Graf vs Arantxa Sánchez Vicario

Date: 8 July 1995
Score: 4-6, 6-1, 7-5

*'I knew the people in the crowd were
getting excited because it was longer and
longer ... but in my mind I just tried to
be calm and concentrate on each point.'*
Arantxa Sánchez Vicario

A TWO-HOUR, two-minute test of wills and of who had the greatest nerve. This was the 14th time Steffi Graf and Arantxa Sánchez Vicario had met in a singles final and this was to be one of the most memorable.

Before the cream had dripped down to the bottom strawberry in the tub, Arantxa had won the first set 6-4. She came out firing on all cylinders and conceded only four points in her service games, taking the first set in a swiftly executed 30 minutes. This was quite a feat and, had she been playing anyone else, you might have thought this was the year the Spanish No. 2 seed was going to be victorious. But Steffi, as always, was the patient opponent. She had experience under her belt, she was the Wimbledon Queen, and she wasn't about to let an excitable youngster take that from her too easily.

Up until that point, the two weeks of Wimbledon had been dubbed tedious by the press. No players or matches had brought with them the spark so often seen during the fortnight, and the words 'stale' and 'predictable' were touted. But they ate their words when Steffi and Arantxa came out onto Centre Court for the final. It was perhaps the perfect setting for it too. Here was Steffi, a reigning champion, looking under threat from a bubbly Spaniard who had become the youngest French Open champion when she was only 17 years old in 1989 and who was looking more at home on a grass court than ever before. She had already knocked out the reigning champion in the semi-final – her Spanish team-mate, Conchita Martínez, 6-3, 6-7, 6-1 – and was looking to take this momentum into the final and give herself the chance to win her first ever Wimbledon title.

But Steffi was on a 32-match winning streak coming into the final and most pundits would have put money on the idea that she would simply steamroll her way to the trophy. Besides, when these two had gone head-to-head, the stats were in Steffi's favour; she had won 28 to Arantxa's eight. So before a shot had even been played, the final looked likely to go the same way as the rest of the tournament – predictably predictable.

But all of that changed the moment Arantxa took the first set. Suddenly the plucky Spaniard with the tremendous court coverage looked like she was going to cause an upset and perhaps, just perhaps, the crowd would be in for a rollercoaster ride. It wasn't unusual for Steffi to find herself on the back foot; she played with a confidence that rarely allowed for nerves when she went behind in the first set, and this time was no different. Steffi found her rhythm, got her powerful forehand back on track and, combined with her relentless groundstrokes to which Arantxa had no answer, secured a relatively quick and painless 6-1 second-set win. So it was one set all. Again, by most standards, nothing unusual in that. Given the ease with which Steffi had won that second set, it seemed likely that the third set would play out in much the same way and the commentators were again expecting a predictable final set, with the five-time champion looking ready to clinch her sixth title.

But Arantxa was in no mood to give up and wasn't going to go down without a fight. This was a meeting of athleticism, sheer grit and force and no one was going to give away any easy points. When the score in the final set was tied at 5-5, the anticipation and excitement in the crowd was bursting on to the court. The cheers and shouts were ringing out, as if each cry of encouragement could provide that crucial bit of help for each player. The final had come alive and the match was as nerve-racking to watch as any sporting final could be. The rallies were long, the excitement heart-stopping, and the 11th game lasted almost 20 minutes as Arantxa battled to hold serve after 13 deuces. She reached game point seven times before Steffi, who kept piling on the pressure, finally managed to break her serve. The game had no fewer than 32 points and it ended with Arantxa finding the net after a leaping forehand smash by Steffi. The wind had gone from the Spaniard's sails.

Steffi might have been injured and, in her own words, 'held together by bits of tape here and there', but she went on to win her service game and the final set 7-5. She had earned her sixth Wimbledon title through her stubbornness and strength, but as both exhausted players reached the net at the end, they embraced in acknowledgement of what they had both just put themselves through. Steffi also made sure that Arantxa got the chance to briefly share a hold of the trophy at the presentation ceremony afterwards, signalling that it could have gone to either player that day. Arantxa never did win a Wimbledon title, although she did reach the finals the following year – but was beaten again by, you guessed it, Steffi.

23

Maria Sharapova vs Serena Williams

Date: 3 July 2004
Score: 6-1, 6-4

'I'm sorry I had to take this trophy from you for one year, I'm sure we're gonna be here many more times and fight for the trophy again.' Maria Sharapova

A RARE afternoon of sun and gentle breeze on Centre Court set the scene for the Ladies' Singles final in 2004. It was as if there needed to be a little extra light shining on the grass court that day, to mark the remarkable match that was about to unfold.

Young Russian star Maria Sharapova was the third-youngest female player ever to reach the final at Wimbledon (Lottie Dodd and Martina Hingis before her), and the crowd took to their feet to welcome her to the grand occasion of a Wimbledon final, and of course to celebrate the return of two-time defending champion, Serena Williams.

If you were going to bet on the final, chances are you might have favoured the No. 1 seed, Serena, who took to Wimbledon like the proverbial duck to water and who had conquered anything and everyone in the past few years of the women's game. But the young teenager from Siberia, the frozen wastelands of Russia, brought with her the power and might of someone who seemed to have been a star of the tennis stage for far longer than her actual four appearances. Refreshingly unnerved by the occasion, it was clear from the first set that Maria's tennis style was fearless. From 1-1 in the first set, Serena did not win another game until the opener of the second set. Following a mixture of unforced errors on Serena's part and an array of meaty groundstrokes and two-handed backhand returns of service from Maria, Serena was knocked well and truly off her stride – and out of the first set. And all in under 30 minutes.

If you were to suspect that a 17-year-old playing against a formidable two-time champion might crack under the pressure, you would have been wrong ... The 13th seed didn't lose a service game until the opening game of the second set and it looked like perhaps a comeback from the defending champion might be on the cards. Serena knew that if she won this match she would be the first player since Steffi Graf in 1993 to hold on to her Wimbledon crown for three consecutive years.

The power from the back of the court was phenomenal from both players, but her ambidextrous qualities and her intensity for someone so young gave Maria the edge. The dramatic way this final was shaping up gave the crowd an unbelievable lesson in challenge and defiance, and the grunts from both players were equalled by the deafening roars of joy from a crowd who knew they were witnessing an epic spectacle.

When Maria broke Serena's serve in the ninth game of the second set, the end seemed nigh. It had been Serena's final bout of aggression and she had thrown all she had at the Russian – serves over 100mph and whipping passing shots – as she managed to fight off three break points in a 14-point game. But when she faced the fourth break point and Maria produced a return filled with utter conviction and power, it was all too much. In a bid to reach the devastating return, Serena slipped and fell to the ground, losing the point and the game. Maria had broken her serve and her heart, and was now serving for the Championship at 5-4.

Not even the pressure of serving against the defending champion in the grand surroundings of Centre Court was too much for Maria. When Serena pummelled a shot into the net when facing Championship point, Maria threw her racket in the air and sank to her knees in tears. It was a reminder of the weight that she carried on her shoulders; this was the first time a Russian player would be crowned

Wimbledon Ladies' champion. She had emerged on the international tennis stage in a blaze of glory and, given her youthfulness – coupled with what she had just achieved – it was no wonder that she buried her face in her hands as the shock of victory was so emotionally overwhelming. As the crowd stood in a deafening ovation, Maria wanted to hug just one person. In a move that Pat Cash first performed back in 1987 – the year Maria was born – she climbed into the stands to embrace her father, Yuri. He raced to meet her, embracing his young daughter in a huge bear hug, goofily grinning up to the skies in a look that only a proud father could pull off.

She wanted to ring her mum to tell her the good news and, in a move that left the Duke Of Kent being asked to wait and the presentation ceremony running over, she tried several times to connect the call to her mother, Yelena, who was in Florida.

As the giggling and excitable Maria accepted the trophy and apologised for taking it from Serena, the press sensed an air of bitterness between the two. In fact, they played a major part in fuelling the rivalry between the two players over the following years. Yet Maria only won one more match against Serena, the same year she won at Wimbledon, out of a further 22 meetings. It seemed that losing to Maria in the final of what should have been her third Wimbledon title meant more to Serena than she first let on. It was reported that she was heard 'bawling guttural sobs' at losing in the final. Maria wrote in her autobiography that she suspected Serena hated the idea that she had overheard her crying, and also revealed: 'Not long after the tournament [Wimbledon], I heard Serena told a friend – who then told me – "I will never lose to that little b***h again."' Prophetic? It would seem so.

24

Stefan Edberg vs Boris Becker

Date: 8 July 1990
Score: 6-2, 6-2, 3-6, 3-6, 6-4

*'It's not as easy as it looks from the outside;
it's a Wimbledon final and everything is
just a little bit more difficult than normal.'*
Boris Becker

LIKE OLD friends reunited in a familiar setting, there
was a touch of déjà vu about the Men's Singles final when
Stefan Edberg and Boris Becker walked out onto Centre
Court in the summer of 1990. It was their third meeting
here. Becker was the defending champion, having won
the previous year in three sets, and two years ago it
was Edberg who claimed victory, beating his German
opponent in four sets. This year, for the first time in
eight years of Men's Singles finals, there was going to be
a fifth-set decider.

Here was Edberg, a naturally gifted grass-court player
who was the master serve and volleyer and rarely seen in

a flap, up against Becker, an immensely powerful server who threw himself across the court and wasn't afraid to bring emotions into his game. It felt like Groundhog Day as the pair came onto Centre Court, but historical rivalry is something we thrive on – the to and fro of two old foes battling it out brings a sense of fond familiarity. Of course, it is exciting to watch new players and see them develop, but there is something special and comforting about watching the familiar faces battling it out on court. The Borg/McEnroe matches, the Navratilova/Evert clashes, the Federer/Nadal trilogies ... It's tradition, right? And like every good tradition, you understand the basics of what is about to happen, but there is always a twist to proceedings.

And so to the 1990 final, which was like a tornado pulsating through court as the pair brought out the best in one another in an emotional display of championship tennis. It didn't start off well for Becker. Edberg could have been playing with one hand behind his back in the first two sets and still won convincingly. Becker appeared unfocused and uninterested in what was happening around him. Edberg won the first set in just 29 minutes, getting off to the sort of start that dreams are made of. The second set went pretty much the same way; 27 minutes of play and another set ticked off for Edberg. Becker won just ten points in that second set as Edberg, fired up from his maiden-set victory, continued his clinic of crushing volleys and juggernaut serves. Their rallies were lasting no more than two or three shots.

'My granny can play better than you!' came one cry from the crowd towards the German former champion. This may have been a slight overreaction towards a three-time Wimbledon champion, but clearly something wasn't quite right. Becker later revealed in his autobiography that he had been taking sleeping pills, which had been prescribed to him, and had taken one the night before the big final. 'I was an idiot. I thought, "If I stay up now until the final I'll be too tired," so I took one more. By 11 o'clock – the final was at two – I was so sleepy. I wanted to wake up; I couldn't warm up because the time was so short.'

Tired or not, something seemed to kick into gear for Becker towards the end of the second set and, as the third set got underway, he proved that this wasn't going to be a complete whitewash and embarrassment. He adjusted his swing, hit an array of backhanded return winners and looked more fired up than he had for the first hour of play. The change had an immediate effect and he was back in the match. Winning the third set and then the fourth left many people wondering whether someone had just been impersonating him at the beginning. Had the No. 2 seed just been toying with Edberg the whole time or was he mirroring a similar comeback of a former champion, Henri Cochet in 1927 (see Match 7), who went on to win after going two sets down? Whatever had happened in the first two sets, the crowd were now watching a new match, and the score was now tied at 2-2.

Edberg went 3-1 down in the final set and, having been two sets in front, felt like another victory was slipping away from him. Becker had hauled himself back from humiliation and it now looked like Edberg would be unable to stop his momentum. Two double faults didn't help his cause, but it wasn't over yet. 'I started to think a little bit,' confirmed Edberg. 'I got my strength back and my fighting spirit.'

After breaking back in a stream of dipping returns, and with Becker himself now double-faulting, Edberg's fighting spirit was indeed in full swing. He sent Becker skidding and tumbling with a series of cross-court stingers and maintained momentum to bring the set score level at 4-4. But that wasn't the most remarkable thing. Edberg was fired up and showing emotion (yep, the crowd couldn't believe it either; who even knew he was capable?) as he grappled back to gain the control he enjoyed in the first two sets. When Becker missed an easy return from an Edberg lob, the joyful cry from the Swede vibrated around the court (again, this was probably more astonishing than his comeback). He won the last two games with more emotional displays than we'd seen from him in his whole career, and when Becker hit a return that went long, the match was all over. Edberg launched a ball into the crowd and the two competitors shared a long hug. Game, set and match to the silent (apart from this short-lived episode) but deadly one.

25

Martina Navratilova vs Chris Evert

Date: 7 July 1978
Score: 2-6, 6-4, 7-5

*'Once you start believing in yourself,
anything is possible. Once you start believing
in yourself, your dreams take shape. The
more you believe, the more you achieve.'*
Martina Navratilova

THE PREVIOUS year had been a time of British celebration when Virginia Wade lifted the trophy and was crowned Wimbledon Queen, while the actual Queen, who presented her with the trophy, celebrated her Silver Jubilee. This year was quite a different story. Virginia had been knocked out in the semi-final to No. 1 seed Chris Evert, who was now hoping to make it a third victory at Wimbledon. Evert had been the top seed for 138 out of the 140 weeks that the WTA's computer ranking system had been up and running. She had been the champion in 1974 and 1976 and was therefore on course for another year-on year-off victory. By contrast, this was Martina's first Wimbledon Singles final appearance, and she was nervous. She had, up until that final, been more of a fan than a rival to Chris, whose poster had adorned the wall of the tennis club near Prague where Martina spent so many hours practising.

The admiration Martina had for Chris took her from fan to friend to team-mate as they teamed up to win the Wimbledon Ladies' Doubles in 1976. Now Martina wanted to go solo and prove her worth as a singles finalist, taking advantage of Chris's four-month holiday at the beginning of the year to win 37 straight matches – including a win against Chris in the Wimbledon warm-up tournament at Eastbourne when she saved two match points to win in the third set. It looked like Czechoslovakian Martina, who had defected to the United States in 1975, was beginning to fulfil her enormous professional potential, even though she was facing personal heartache and loneliness. On defecting to America, she was forced to leave her parents and sister back in Prague after her home country stripped her of her citizenship. It wasn't until 1981 that she officially became a US citizen, and then, in 2008, she regained Czech citizenship. So at the time of the Wimbledon final, she was, as one newspaper reported, 'the girl without a country'.

In a sure sign of nerves, Martina misjudged her turn and curtsy to the Royal Box as she came out onto Centre Court, looked like she was gulping in air like it was going out of fashion before the match had even begun, and then, looking quite frantic in her style of play, rushed through the first games in a combination of errors and frenzied play. It all seemed to be going the way of the pre-match predictions, with Chris taking the first set easily and setting the tone for what many believed would be the second and final set. Job done. But then something happened in the second set to change the balance of the whole match. Martina began to use her persistence and relentless aggression to her advantage and, when the second set went into the sixth game, it seemed all Martina needed was a blow to the head to focus her attention. Yes, really. The crowd couldn't hide their gasps as Martina – who had rushed to the net, believing Chris was going to hit a cross-court pass – took a forehand shot to her left temple. Chris ran to the net to check her friend was OK, while Martina decided to play the guilt card, dramatically staggering a little before falling to one knee, smiling and assuring Chris she was indeed OK. In fact, she was better than OK.

It seemed the blow to the head was all she needed to step up a gear and get herself back in the game, saving three break points and holding her serve. At 5-4 in the second set she was giving as good as she got, making the final rally of the set a battle of wills as the players matched each other's baseline shots before Martina proved she had the stamina to get the win. Now it was one set all and it seemed, to the commentators at least, that it could go either way.

'I knew Martina had it in her,' admitted one Centre Court spectator. 'I remember she looked into the crowd at one point, like she was searching for someone in particular, but I wonder if she was imagining her family being there and watching her. I think she wanted to win for them, it gave her an edge.'

In contrast, Chris was looking like she lacked the appetite for the title. The night before, she had been out with her new boyfriend, British player and her future husband, John Lloyd. It was only their second date and Chris admitted later that she had been more eager to spend time with a new exciting friend than fret over facing Martina on Centre Court. It was a revelation that spoke volumes. In the final set she went 0-2 down before coming back at Martina to win the next 4 games.

The pendulum was swinging back and forth, each player giving a display of contrasting playing styles, grit and determination. But it was Martina, perhaps after the shot to her head or perhaps because she sensed her good friend had other things on her mind, that forced her to step up her game. As Chris hesitated, Martina grew stronger and won 12 of the last 13 points for the title of Wimbledon champion. As her last shot – a beautifully executed half-volley – passed under Chris's racket, all Martina could do was let out a shriek before rushing to the net to hug her good friend. For 102 minutes it was a final filled with multiple changes of fortune, but in the end the rookie had beaten her idol.

At the presentation ceremony, Martina – slowly getting over her astonishment at winning – looked every inch the champion with a beaming smile. Similarly, Chris looked rather happy – despite being the runner-up – perhaps in a nod to the new direction of her personal life. The Duchess of Kent asked Martina about her family as she presented her with the trophy and was told that her parents had managed to travel to the German border where they had been able to watch the match. And it was the first on a very long list of finals they would watch their daughter compete in (this was the first of a record-breaking nine Wimbledon titles). A great number of those games would be against her old foe, Chris (they actually played each other 80 times in total), as she began to dominate the women's game, especially in the art of serve and volley, a style few could thwart or ever match.

26

Stan Smith vs Ilie Năstase

Date: 9 July 1972
Score: 4-6, 6-3, 6-3, 4-6, 7-5

'80 per cent guts and a little luck.'
Stan Smith

SOMETIMES RAIN puts a damper on the spirit of an occasion, and at other times it adds to the drama and tension of a match. When it came to the 1972 final, the good old British weather played a big part in the thrilling All England Club final. For the first time in the history of the Championships, the Men's Singles final was to be played on a Sunday. This was no longer a day of rest, this was a day of guts and glory.

The two finalists were as different as two men can possibly be. Smith was a strait-laced American from the US Army, and Ilie Năstase was an emotional, erratic but entertaining Romanian. Both had the skill set, yet each used those skills in a vastly different manner. The underrated Smith was able to produce master shots that

135

few had seen before, and wasn't limited to his serve-and-volley game; he could hit delicate drop shots when required or even more gentle, yet deadly, stop volleys. Năstase was unpredictable on court, spontaneous and creative with his shots, making him an opponent who was difficult to read but would sometimes find it hard to concentrate. In this instance, he rose to the occasion. He put aside his short-tempered, show-off persona to produce tennis that would be studied in years to come as being as close to perfection as you might ever get to see. His anticipation and speed around the court allowed him to turn several seemingly lost balls into winners.

For both players, the road to the final had not been particularly strenuous, Năstase perhaps losing a few more sets along the way than Smith. But equally Smith was a hugely underrated player. The previous year he had lost in the final to John Newcombe, who lifted his third Wimbledon trophy. This year, just two weeks before the Championships, Smith had lost out to a little-known British player at Queen's Club, and he had been playing quite timidly as he advanced through the stages of the Championships.

But now the stage was set, the wait was over, the skies were clear and the crowds were ready. If anything, prolonging the Men's final simply added to the excitement of the occasion. The two men strode out onto Centre Court to the cheers of the crowd. At 6ft 4in and blond,

Smith was lean and poised. Năstase was shorter, with the air of a man who knew he was supremely gifted and ambitious. As play got underway, it was clear the players shared two things in common: the ambition to win and the guts to prove they were worthy of victory.

The first test of Smith's resolve came in the fifth game of the first set, when he was serving at 40-15. He double-faulted and then Năstase hit a spectacular running return, taking the play to deuce. Smith managed to fend off three break points to win the game. He very nearly broke Năstase in the following game and must have had it in his mind that he could have been serving at 4-2 rather than 3-3. At 4-4, Năstase finally broke him, dipping his returns so that Smith had to play defensive volley shots that were easy to answer.

When the Romanian won his serve and then broke Smith again in the first game of the second set, Smith changed gear. He had previously told the press that he was getting better as this Wimbledon progressed, and it was this final that proved his point. Get better he did, as he won a solid three games in a row and the second set 6-3.

Năstase again broke him early in the third set and, at 0-2, Smith upped his game again, winning another three consecutive games and going on to take the third set. The crowd were getting a heavy dose of drama for a Sunday, and a few were even touting it as the greatest final they had witnessed so far. And it was far from over. In the fourth set the players were tied at four games all, when Năstase replied to Smith's recent set win with a running forehand pass that Smith was only able to watch. The Romanian had made his comeback and it was two sets all.

The fifth set was going to be the test of both men. They battled back and forth with a battery of classic shots which, watching from the stands, looked almost impossible to make and to return, yet both men kept hitting and returning them over and over again.

Năstase was piling on the pressure and, when Smith served for the fifth game at 40-0, something in the Romanian exploded. Năstase pulled out some outrageous shots – including a whipped topspin lob off the backhand that he made look, frankly, easy – and Smith suddenly found himself trying to save five game points. It took a diving stop volley, a drop shot, a forehand smash right into the corner and a big serve to do so … but he did. 'That game was crucial,' Smith said later. 'I slowed myself right down and took a couple of deep breaths.'

The players were pulling off punishing shots over and over again, and the constant cheers from the crowd reflected what a dramatic and entertaining final this was. When it went 5-4 in Smith's favour, and Năstase was serving at 15-40, he managed to fend off two match points with a cutting volley and a punishing backhand.

About ten minutes later it was 6-5 in Smith's favour, with Năstase serving at 40-0. 'At that point I figured he was going to win his game, I'll just keep hitting a couple of balls, and they went in!' recalled Smith. 'And then it got to deuce.'

Năstase served to Smith's forehand and he returned with a winner. It was match point again for Smith. Centre Court was eerily silent. Smith returned Năstase's serve with what he intended as an overhead lob, but it fell short and Năstase jumped up for an overhead smash in response. This was a shot Năstase had played successfully and repeatedly throughout the match, but at this crucial time, when it mattered most, the ball fell into the net. It was all over.

'I suddenly realised I had won Wimbledon,' revealed Smith. 'I threw my racket 40 feet in the air and I jumped over the net to congratulate him for a good match. I couldn't believe it.'

The crowd were euphoric and filled with immense respect and admiration for both players. In two hours and 43 minutes, those gathered around that significant little block of grass had witnessed the crowning of a new Wimbledon champion. When he came into the press room, drenched in sweat and champagne, the relief was clear. 'Never in doubt,' grinned Smith. 'Never in doubt.'

Steffi Graf vs Martina Navratilova

Date: 2 July 1988
Score: 5-7, 6-2, 6-1

*'This is the end of a chapter, passing
the torch if you want to call it that.'*
Martina Navratilova

IT WAS a suitably regal setting for the dethroning of an
eight-time world champion: the Royal Box was a Who's
Who of champions, with the likes of Kitty Godfree,
Angela Mortimer and Alice Marble all enjoying the
warm sunshine. There was an air of anticipation about
the action that was due to unfold before them, and much
talk of what was set to be a historic match – if anyone
was likely to put an end to current Wimbledon champion
Navratilova's six consecutive titles, it was going to be
19-year-old Steffi Graf.

SW19 was like a home to Martina and she was now
looking to make history by adding a ninth Wimbledon
win to her trophy cabinet, thereby surpassing Helen Wills

Moody as the Queen of Centre Court. But if death and taxes are the only two certainties in life, two things can often be relied on when it comes to Wimbledon finals: the English weather and a big upset. The British climate can make or break a champion – delays in play can help you regroup mentally or stop you flat when you are playing your most perfect tennis.

This final had it all, including a teenager with a point to prove. Steffi Graf was 12 years younger than the seasoned champion she was playing, but she wasn't going to be overwhelmed by the occasion or her surroundings. Not that she needed to prove anything to the Wimbledon contingent; she was already on her way to a Grand Slam year, having won the Australian Open in January and the French Open a few weeks before Wimbledon. If she won here, at the grand dame of Grand Slam events, she would need just the US Open title in September to complete her Grand Slam year. But she was also on course for a Golden Slam, with the Olympics being held in October in Seoul. This was the first time tennis had been included in the Games for 64 years and it was an opportunity too good to miss for the young German.

But first things first, and back to the morning of the final. The weather looked distinctly dubious, but couldn't dampen the enthusiasm of either finalist or the excitable Centre Court crowd. If we were betting people, our money would have been on Martina that day. Riding high with confidence and buoyed by the chance to make history, she had also beaten Steffi the previous year at the All England Club. This was her turf. It would take something (or someone) spectacular to make her give up her throne. But all good things, as they say, must come to an end. Perhaps Martina was consumed with trying to prove that she was still good enough to compete against a new wave of young stars, but change was definitely in the air. For the first time, none of the players competing in this year's tournament was using a wooden racket. They were now history, gone, forgotten. For Martina, would this prove to be an ominous portent of change?

The match began in much the way commentators and fans had predicted; Martina was aiming to exploit Steffi's weakness, which was her backhand. The only problem was that it was still a lot better than most, and while Martina did indeed slice her serve and groundstrokes to Steffi's backhand in the first set, it wasn't as easy as she would have liked. But the eight-time Wimbledon winner did what she set out to do and took the first set 7-5.

When Martina broke Steffi's serve in the second set to go 2-0 up, it looked like the young teen, shoulders sagging, would succumb to the more rounded game of the old master. She had now lost six consecutive games and was cross. She later admitted that the first set had left her feeling furious because she wasn't showing how well she could play.

So as the rain clouds mustered over SW19, Steffi made her move. After hitting two return winners with her forehand, Steffi started to turn the tables on Martina, who went on to lose her serve.* Steffi's forceful serves and returns picked up and she won the next nine games. She had tied scores with Martina by winning the second set 6-2 and was now ahead in the final set. The comeback was real and her forehands were relentless – cross-court, down the line, Graf would clobber it away from all areas of the court.

It looked like Martina might get a reprieve as a few raindrops began to fall, but the crowd, sensing predator Steffi closing in on her prey, started to boo when they felt Martina was stalling and stopping frequently mid-serve to wipe the rain from her glasses. Martina broke Steffi in the fourth game of the set but, as the drops of rain turned heavier and stopped play, her own momentum was lost. The players came back out onto court 44 minutes later, but it was Steffi who had the winning glint in her eye. Sure enough, Steffi held her serve. In order to win the Championship she would have to break Martina's serve, which she managed to do on her own merit (a whipped backhand return), through Martina's error (two double faults) and with a little luck (a fortuitous net shot that left Martina helpless). But no one could dispute that the teenager was a worthy winner. Steffi had won 12 of the last 13 games and was described by one commentator as 'shrinking the court with her legs'.

An ecstatic Steffi threw her racket into the crowd, something she had done the previous year when she won the French Open for the first time. She had taken on the mighty champion and won, showing a level of grit and determination you might expect to see in someone much older and more experienced. You could, in fact, call her a Graffter. The only point in this final when she did show a few nerves was when she had to be shown how to hold the trophy to the cheering crowd and photographers. If Martina could take any solace as she clutched the smaller runners-up plate to her chest, it was that she had, in her own words, handed over the mantle to a player whose Grand Slam ambition was as fierce and formidable as her topspin forehand. Steffi did indeed go on to complete the Golden Slam that year – the only player ever to claim that accolade, before or since.

*Insert 'nerve'?

28

Suzanne Lenglen and Elizabeth Ryan vs Dorothea Lambert Chambers and Ethel Thomson Larcombe

Date: 16 July 1919
Score: 4-6, 7-5, 6-3

*'If you are skilled and well drilled in
discipline and sportsmanship, you are
bound to benefit in the strife of the world.'*
Lawn Tennis for Ladies, published 1910

IF YOU hold a record number of wins at Wimbledon at any stage of your professional career, chances are that at some point, however great the number and however impressive the feat, someone will beat it eventually. And so it was for the formidable doubles duo of Suzanne Lenglen and Elizabeth 'Bunny' Ryan. Both ladies had met each other in the singles competition many times, with Suzanne always winning and Bunny failing to secure any major singles title. Bunny is affectionately known

as one of the greatest players of her era never to win a
Wimbledon singles title (or any, for that matter). But
when the pair joined forces, they were an unstoppable
duo. So unstoppable in fact that American star Bunny
went on to hold the record for the most doubles titles at
Wimbledon – a staggering 19, including six wins with
Suzanne.

Bunny and Suzanne paired up for the first time on
the Wimbledon doubles stage in 1919, in the year that
Suzanne won her first singles title. She had beaten Bunny
in the semi-final, 6-4, 7-5, and went on to face the might of
the seven-time champion, Dorothea Lambert Chambers.
It was an epic final filled with drama. Suzanne's father
threw sugar lumps soaked in brandy onto the court to
help his daughter, while King George V and Queen Mary
watched in awe at the ambitious, often extravagant, shots
played by the young French girl.

The fact that she came onto Centre Court (at its home
on Worple Road in those days) in a loose-fitting white
dress with sleeves above the elbow and a hemline above
the knee drew gasps from the crowd. Where were the
layers of petticoats? Where were the tight-fitting corset
and blouse? But we digress. The year of her first triumph
as a singles star saw her joining forces with Bunny at the
beginning of their record-breaking partnership. While it
was a maiden voyage onto the doubles court for Suzanne,
Bunny had competed in 1914 with English player, Agnes

Morton. Due to World War I, it would be another five years before Bunny returned to the doubles court, but this time with the woman who denied her a singles trophy at her side.

Bunny and Suzanne faced Suzanne's singles opponent, Dorothea, and her English partner, Ethel Thomson Larcombe. As the crowds swelled to watch the play, the All England Club knew it would no longer be able to hold the Championships at the humble grounds and that a new venue would be needed to deal with the growing surge of spectators. The pair didn't get off to the best start against their British opponents. In fact, Dorothea and Ethel were one set up and 5-4 in the second set before the magic began to happen. When the British duo went 30-0 up, two points away from victory, Bunny and Suzanne fought back. As it happened, they were a force just coming into their stride.

Both of them were strong volleyers, with Suzanne quick enough to go back for lobs when they were both at the net, but Bunny preferred the baseline. A few early mistakes cost them that first set. This match is significant because of that loss. This was the only set they lost in their six doubles wins at Wimbledon. Let's just say that again, shall we? The only set they lost in their six Championship wins!

With Bunny's strong volley and lethal drop shots and Suzanne's forceful groundstrokes, the pair seemed unstoppable and their style of play formidable. While their opponents, Dorothea and Ethel, played according to the largely uniform one-up (Ethel) one-back (Dorothea) formation, Bunny and Suzanne were both equally comfortable at the net or baseline. Seeing both players at the net was a relatively new occurrence, but its effectiveness was clear. After watching Suzanne and Bunny play in this formation, other pairs adopted their style, enabling them to be both attacking and defensive on court. In the end, for the second time that week, poor Dorothea saw the Championship almost within her grasp only to be denied yet again. Matching up against Suzanne and Bunny was hard for any opponents and, although Dorothea drove well from the baseline, Ethel struggled against the severity of Suzanne's attack.

Suzanne went on to achieve the treble the following year, when she won the Ladies' Singles, the Doubles and the Mixed Doubles, repeating that feat in 1922 and 1925. While Bunny never did achieve singles success, she was unstoppable in the doubles and mixed doubles, winning 26 Grand Slam titles in those combined events.

And what of Bunny's record of 19 doubles titles? She readily admitted that she did not want to live to see her record of 19 Wimbledon titles broken and, in a bittersweet twist of fate, her wish came true. In 1979, long after Bunny had hung up her wooden racket, Billie Jean King was taking part in the Ladies' Doubles final with her partner, Martina Navratilova. Billie had matched Bunny's record of 19 wins. If she won the final that year at Wimbledon, she would beat it. The day before that potential record-breaking final, Bunny was strolling in the grounds of the All England Club and collapsed, passing away shortly afterwards. So she never did live to see her record, or her heart, get broken, as the following day Billy took her 20th doubles title.

29

Kitty McKane vs Helen Wills

Date: 5 July 1924
Score: 4-6, 6-4, 6-4

*'I love the feeling of hitting the ball hard,
the pleasure of a rally. It is these things
that make tennis the delightful game it is.'*
Helen Wills

WHEN FIVE-TIME defending champion Suzanne Lenglen retired from the 1924 tournament due to ill health, her semi-final opponent, Kathleen 'Kitty' McKane was suddenly propelled to the final. Would she be the first English woman to win the Championship since 1914? Standing in her way was new US champion, Helen Wills. Young Helen was a superstar in the making, adored by her country and coming to Wimbledon for the first time, so expectations fell squarely on her shoulders. She was the new sweetheart of the game, but how would she fare in Blighty?

The crowds gathered on that balmy July day were, of course, rooting for their own, especially as Kitty had lost out in the final the year before – to Lenglen in just two sets. The 9,000 seated spectators on Centre Court – together with those 1,800 who were standing – were in for a treat. It's also worth noting that it had only been two years since the grand new Centre Court had been opened, and by 1924 it was clear that more expansion would be needed and that another 'show court' would be required. Court No. 1 had originally been designated as a hard court after the All England Club moved to Church Road in 1922, but it became the second main grass court instead when it opened in 1924, with accommodation for 3,250 spectators.

English fans had high expectations. They wanted a post-war champion to celebrate, but as with any good battle, our hero's chances looked bleak when Helen took the first set with relative ease. The teenager was known for practising with male counterparts, playing a relentless game that would eventually wear down and break her opponents. And it certainly looked like Kitty, struggling to get into the match, was going to surrender to the young American.

After Helen went one set up and 4-1 up in the second, you could forgive her for practising her victory pose. Her win looked almost certain, with Kitty showing no signs of making a comeback. When Helen came to serve in the sixth game and went 40-15 up, Kitty's fate looked sealed. A few spectators hung their heads in defeat.

There was no doubting that Helen looked unbreakable and was inches away from victory. But then came the cavalry. Or the comeback charge. Or the steady and steely English nerve perhaps. Call it what you will, but what happened next was one of the biggest fightbacks the All England Club had ever witnessed. We all love an underdog, and whether it was the cheering crowd, the thought of another defeat, or the realisation that if she didn't beat Helen this year she might not get another chance (Helen was clearly on her way to becoming a class ahead of any female player), Kitty's meow turned into a roar. She wasn't going down without a fight and, being so close to defeat, she had everything to play for. Many thought she had left it too late to attack, but attack she did. Her aggressive volleys and agility around the court stepped up a gear and she won the next five games to even the match.

Now at one set all, and with everything to play for in the third, what looked to be a clear-cut American victory only a brief time ago was now anyone's game. If either player was now getting nervous, they didn't give anything away. It was as much a battle of wills and strength of character as forehand drives and lobs; as much a battle of pride and passion as volleys and serves. Kitty's net play was unbeatable and, at 3-3 in the final set, it was to help carry her to a lead of 5-3. Helen won her service game to go 4-5 and now it was up to Kitty to win or lose. She was showing every spectator, commentator and athlete the true meaning of holding one's nerve. And she did.

It was a steely steadiness that gave her victory that day, and the chance for the nation to celebrate an English winner – a much-needed morale boost. Kitty's victory marked the only time Helen would lose a game at the Championships in a further eight appearances. She won the Wimbledon Ladies' title when she came back in 1927 and then again in 1928, 1929, 1930, 1932, 1933, 1935 and 1938, when she was 32 years old. It was an achievement that was only surpassed, years later, by Martina Navratilova in 1990. As if to prove that defeat at Wimbledon was a pure one-off, less than ten days later Helen was in Paris for the Olympic Games, winning gold in both the Women's Doubles and Women's Singles. Tennis was then dropped from the Olympics until 1988 – the year another trailblazing star, Steffi Graf, claimed a Golden Slam.

Of course, no one knew that then; they only knew that they had an English woman as their Wimbledon champion. Queen of the court, Kitty went on to win the Ladies' final again in 1926, and the opening day of the Jubilee Championship saw her presented to King George V and Queen Mary. That year she went on to win the Mixed Doubles with her husband, Leslie Godfree. They became the first and only husband and wife team to win the Mixed Doubles title at Wimbledon.

The final against Helen was perhaps her greatest win. Coming back after being so far behind showed true courage and spirit, highlighting the idea that in any given moment we have two options – step forward or step back. If you are ever unsure about overcoming a particular hurdle, we suggest you channel your inner Kitty!

30

Evonne Goolagong Cawley vs Chris Evert

Date: 5 July 1980
Score: 6-1, 7-6

*'My dream growing up was to win
Wimbledon, which was fantastic when it
happened in 1971. However, I loved playing
after having Kelly, I really wanted to win
again.'* Evonne Goolagong Cawley

THE 1980 Championships brought a series of firsts –
fitting for a new decade of tennis and for a new wave of
fans and supporters at SW19. It was the 80s, the dawn of a
fresh wave of female empowerment, and no one embodied
that more than Evonne Goolagong Cawley, who became
the first mother to win the Ladies' Singles title in 66
years.

Defending champion, Martina Navratilova, who had
beaten Billie Jean King in the quarter-final that year, was
beaten by her arch-rival Chris Evert in the semi. That had
been an epic battle between the two, swinging first in the

defending champion's favour when she took the first set 6-4, before Chris fought back by winning 6-4 and then 6-2 in the final set. There was to be a new Queen of Wimbledon to start the new decade, and why shouldn't that be, for the first time in the Open Era, a mother?

The 80s brought a new sense of drama, too, with television being used to heighten the excitement of the Championships, creating rivalries for viewers and ensuring scheduling of matches was of the utmost importance. The Ladies' final was moved from a Friday to a Saturday, and the Men's final to a Sunday. The move was made to increase worldwide television appeal and bring a new audience to Wimbledon – up until that point, it had been the only major championship to hold the men's final on a Saturday. In 1980 the prize money for the Ladies' winner was £18,000, but by 1989 this had increased to a whopping £171,000; still way behind the Men's prize (it wasn't equal until 2007), but it showed just how much the money in the game was increasing.

The Ladies' final was between two players who knew what it meant to be a winner at Wimbledon. Evonne had to delve deeper in her memory to recall the last time she lifted the trophy, in 1971. She had reached the final in both 1972 and 1975, but lost to Billie Jean King on both occasions, and in 1976 she lost to Chris in a heartbreaking third set. Chris, who was number one in the rankings from 1975 to 1982, had won in 1974 and 1976 (and she would also win in 1981, the year Catherine McTavish would become the first female to umpire on Centre Court). In the space of one hour and 33 minutes, the crowd were treated to an exceptional display between two focused rivals. The match also featured the first tie-break set to determine the champion.

If becoming a mother had influenced Evonne's playing style, it had made her more fearless (she had previously admitted that she was fed up of being 'runner-up') and right from the first point she was in command of the match. Even though a few commentators didn't credit her with much of a chance in the final, often citing the fact it had been nine years since she had won the title, when she had been an energetic teen, Evonne had a lot to prove. Could she even get close to winning now that she was two years shy of 30 and a mother? In contrast, Chris was riding high with confidence, having just come from an exceptional win against Martina Navratilova that proved she was at the top of her game. But it was Evonne who seemed to show her hunger for victory right from the off. She allowed Chris's deadly passing shots to go unchallenged, knowing she could match her cross-court and serving action. She brought Chris into the net several times before sending soft winning lobs over her head. She caught Chris off guard with her sudden bursts of speed and changes of direction, and displayed a confidence in her overheads that was unmatched.

The sun was shining as the battle began, but the previous two weeks had seen unsettled weather that had halted several matches. Interestingly, all of Evonne's matches up to the final had been played in dazzling sunshine, while many of her competitors dealt with 'rain stops play' frustrations. Evonne won the first set in a manner that seemed effortless, taking it 6-1 after breaking Chris early on. The weather did play a small part in the second set when, at 1-1, they had to briefly scuttle off court before returning to an overcast afternoon.

It was the tie-break in the second set that really proved the strength of Evonne's will to win. There were no breaks of serve until Evonne finally overpowered Chris and went 4-3 up after an epic rally. The end was in sight and, when she took the title with her second Championship point, mothers the world over went wild. It would be another decade until Girl Power was in full swing, but out here, on a small patch of grass, Evonne proved that being a mum and a Wimbledon champion could be done. And you can bet that her three-year-old daughter, Kelly, who might not have been watching the match that year, would be watching footage of her mum's victory for years to come.

31

Venus Williams vs Lindsay Davenport

Date: 2 July 2005
Score: 4-6, 7-6, 9-7

*'My motto is "I'm alive" so I can
do anything, so long as I am alive.'*
Venus Williams

YOU RARELY see a photo of a player looking so utterly and completely joyful as Venus Williams after her Wimbledon win in 2005. Think of a child being overwhelmed with excitement and multiply it by 14, Venus's seeding when she entered the Championships that year. She had burst onto the scene to shake up women's tennis five years previously, winning the tournament in 2000 and 2001. Since then, however, she had fallen from the top ten and lost her mojo; according to some critics at the time, being a champion at 17 apparently meant that you were done at 25. It was a sad fall from the top spot for the American. Before Wimbledon she had suffered a humiliating defeat at Roland Garros to an unknown

15-year-old from Bulgaria called Sesil Karatantcheva. Yep, who? Richard Williams's prediction – when Venus first emerged as a champion – that his younger daughter, Serena, who had yet to emerge, was 'meaner' and would therefore be 'greater', seemed to be prophetic. And yet that old chestnut, never underestimate a woman with a point to prove, was about to ring out on the courts of SW19 as Venus entered the tournament with a fire in her belly that wasn't going to be extinguished until she lifted that trophy.

In fact, it didn't come close to being dampened until that final; she didn't drop a set in the entire tournament up to that point – even when she faced the reigning champion, Maria Sharapova, in the semi-final. Maria had beaten her sister the previous year to become Wimbledon's Queen. Whether Venus had a score to settle on her sister's behalf, we couldn't possibly comment, but she sure as hell wasn't going to give her the chance to beat another Williams at this tournament and she defeated the teenager 7-6, 6-1.

Serena had been knocked out in the third round, her earliest exit at any Grand Slam tournament since 1999's French Open. Now there was just fellow American and No. 1 seed Lindsay Davenport standing in Venus's way. As the players came out onto Centre Court, there was a sense that this would be Lindsay's match. After all, she had been No. 1 for the previous ten months. But Venus had steamrolled her way to the final with tremendous displays of athleticism and power and it would be unwise to discount her now.

Serena, who had flown home, sent emails of support to her big sis and some worthy advice for the final – to fight and keep fighting. It certainly was a battle that was fought until the final point. It was also the longest Ladies' final in history, eclipsing Billie Jean King and Margaret Court's marathon final in 1970, which lasted two hours and 28 minutes. Venus and Lindsay didn't stop for two hours and 45 minutes, an hour longer than the Men's final that year.

Lindsay was a phenomenal player. She had the cleanest strike in the game, and a style based around her groundstrokes, two-handed backhand and solid serve. She was at the peak of her game and deservedly in the No. 1 spot. As the action began, it looked like she would be adding another Wimbledon title to her cabinet, having won in 1999 against the mighty Steffi Graf. She took the first set with relative ease at 6-4 and then served for the Championship at 6-5 in the second set after breaking Venus's serve. Venus was down but not out, and she also had the ability to pull out a breathtaking display of aggression. Not only did she not let Lindsay win a single point in her service game, but she also won the tie-break 7-4, stealing the set from under Lindsay's nose, not to mention the Championship as well. Faced with disaster,

Venus had shown she was able to pull out the stops to halt the slide and alter the course of the final.

The third set became a test of who could suffer a break without letting it destroy them. Lindsay broke first and then Venus broke back. At 30-30 and 5-4 down, Venus double-faulted and had to face down another Championship point, which she did by obliterating a double-handed backhand down the line. No one in the Open Era – not since Helen Wills Moody in 1935, in fact – had saved a Championship point and gone on to win the tournament. When she was asked about that moment after the game, Venus was equally perplexed at how calm she had been. 'I think I was thinking, OK, get my first serve in, then on my groundstrokes keep my head down and stay down and run them all down. I'd like to win without a heart attack and going into cardiac arrest,' she beamed.

The third set lasted 78 minutes in total, the momentum swinging between the players and keeping the crowd on the edge of their seats. Venus went down 6-7 and again stood just two points from being that year's runner-up. But she fought and fought again, levelling the match at 7-7 before breaking and going ahead 8-7 to serve for the Championship.

Now it was Lindsay's turn to face the danger and she was unable to complete the escape act that Venus had managed before her, smashing a forehand into the net.

Venus leapt into the air with a triumphant shout, and Centre Court responded in a similar fashion, feeling they had witnessed an epic game of grit and resilience from two phenomenal players and that a worthy winner had claimed victory. And there was no doubting who the winner was; she was the one beaming from ear to ear as she leapt ecstatically in the air. And who could blame her?

32

Angelique Kerber vs Serena Williams

Date: 14 July 2018
Score: 6-3, 6-3

*'To all the moms out there, I was playing for
you today. And I tried.'* Serena Williams

WHEN CENTRE Court stands to greet the players as
they come out for the first time, there is acknowledgement
that for the next hour or two they will be entertained by
two athletes fighting for the hallowed title of Wimbledon
champion. Time seems to be relative on Centre Court.
Some finals are seemingly endless, taking every ounce of
energy and emotion, while others flash by in the blink of
an eye, such is the power and speed of the action.

When Serena Williams stepped out onto Centre Court
after a two-hour delay owing to a particularly long and
hard-fought Men's semi-final (Rafael Nadal and Novak
Djokovic had to complete their match that had been
halted at 11pm the previous night in compliance with
the tournament rules), she was hoping she would be able

to provide the 14,900 crowd with the show they had come to expect. It was a star-studded affair, too. In the front row of the Royal Box were the Duchess of Cambridge and the Duchess of Sussex, who was one of Serena's close friends, and just behind them sat Billie Jean King, Martina Navratilova, Virginia Wade, Emma Watson and Thandie Newton. There was sports royalty seated amongst the crowd too. Golfing legend Tiger Woods and Formula One champion Lewis Hamilton were also in attendance in Williams's box, as was US *Vogue* editor, Anna Wintour.

For Serena, this was about more than a 24th Grand Slam title and an eighth Wimbledon win to add to her collection. This was about being a woman and a mother in the world of competitive sport. Seeded 25th, Serena was making her comeback here at Wimbledon after becoming a mother for the first time, not quite 11 months before. Let's just say that again, not even 11 months ago. Reaching the final was an incredible physical feat following 13 months of maternity leave and a difficult childbirth that resulted in a horrific list of life-threatening complications, leaving her bedridden for six weeks. She was testing her physical prowess in a return to the sport she loved and had shown incredible strength to make her way through the two weeks of the tournament to get this far. By contrast, No. 11 seed Angelique was looking for her first Wimbledon crown and the accolade of becoming the first German since Steffi Graf to lift the Singles trophy. But this wasn't the first time she had reached the Wimbledon final. In 2016 she faced Serena for the first time and was beaten 7-5, 6-3, giving Serena her seventh title. Now, two years later, six years younger than Serena, and as a player praised for her robust defence, she wasn't looking for history to repeat itself.

It wasn't the best start for Serena. Angelique won the coin toss and chose to receive the mighty Serena serve. And she broke that serve after just three minutes in an astonishing start to the match, sparking a sign of things to come. Angelique's strategy became clear very early on; not to compete with the aces (Serena managed 44 in the match), but to punish Serena physically by moving her from side to side, bringing her forward with drop shots, and getting her on the wrong foot whenever she could. Angelique was strong and unafraid of Serena's powerful groundstrokes, blasting them back with similar force and precision.

Serena broke back in the fourth game to level the set at 2-2 and, with one of the fastest serves of the women's tournament at 125mph, won her service game to go ahead for the first time in the match. Kerber answered back by holding her next service game and then breaking Serena again after a series of double faults and unforced errors from the former champion. Serena was unable to retaliate in the next game, and so went into her service game 3-5 in the first set. At 0-30 down and just two points from conceding the first set, Serena's spirit was being tested. She fought back to win the next two points, squaring the game at 30-all, but when Angelique took the next point and Serena rammed a high backhand into the net, the first set was all over.

The crowd sensed they would need to play their part if the second set was going to go Serena's way, and the cheers of encouragement grew. They wanted to see this match going to a third set, and besides, there was a new wave of support for Serena since she had given birth and spoken so candidly about the problems and difficulties she faced afterwards. Suddenly, to many fans, this was no longer someone who was alien to them, but a real woman with relatable problems.

At 2-2 in the second set, it became clear that Angelique was completely orchestrating the match, dragging Serena around the court, sapping her energy and taking the edge off of her shots. Angelique took command in the sixth game to break again, going 4-2 up and continuing to send Serena charging around the court like a maniac. But in a last-ditch attempt at a response (and a champion's response at that), Serena held her serve at 3-5 down without giving a single point away. But was that momentous game enough to mark a change in fortune? Well, no. By then, at 5-3 and serving for the Championship, Angelique knew she had that extra edge over an exhausted Serena. As she served the match-winning point, Serena's return could only find the net. Overwhelmed with the realisation of what she had done, Angelique crumbled to the ground in utter disbelief, and Serena, ever gracious in defeat, walked around the side of the net to hug and congratulate her younger opponent. The whole of the crowd stood to applaud not just the new Wimbledon champion but also the runner-up, who had come back after having had a baby less than a year ago and produced such a high level of tennis that she had made it to the final, if not the winner's podium. Sue Barker hit the nail on the head when she described Serena, at the presentation ceremony afterwards, as a 'superhero supermum'.

33

Goran Ivanišević vs Tim Henman

Date: 6 July, 7 July, 8 July 2001
Score: 7-5, 6-7, 0-6, 7-6, 6-3

*'When you are a British player and you
are challenging for big titles, and especially
Wimbledon, you either win it or lose it.
There is no in-between.'* Tim Henman

THERE IS hope and there is Henman hope. Never has a player offered so much promise to the British public, but never quite gone the distance. And never has the British public cared so much about someone who filled us with such promise yet ultimately wasn't able to deliver the goods. But Tiger Tim created so much more than just an opportunity to win Wimbledon, and to celebrate a British champion; he created what was the essence of Wimbledon – the chance to savour the game, to appreciate the courage it took to get there and to come together as a nation to support a hero. Never has the All England Club celebrated an oh-so-nearly-champion with such gusto – Henman

Hill and Henmania are testament to his popularity and possibility.

That said, this epic semi-final between No. 6 seed Henman and a man who had entered the tournament unseeded was a frustrating one. This felt like a very real chance for Timmy to do what we all believed (hoped, prayed, dreamed!) he could do – get to his first Wimbledon final.

When Henman triumphed in the quarter-final (7-5, 7-6, 2-6, 7-6) against Roger Federer, who had in turn beaten Pete Sampras, the semi-final scene was set. He would be up against Goran Ivanišević, and elderly ladies could feel success in their water. This was Henman's third semi-final in four years and he was facing a player he had never lost to. Surely this was the year Henman would reach the final. Surely?!

'I don't expect much support. All England is talking about is Henman winning,' revealed Goran Ivanišević. 'There will be a huge pressure, and we'll see who handles it best.' No truer word was spoken, but while the Centre Court crowd were of course rooting for Hero Henman, all would not be lost if the unthinkable (whisper it) happened and Henman lost. Ivanišević was a man who had all but given up tennis at the beginning of this year and was granted a wild-card entry more out of sentimentality rather than form. No one was expecting him to progress to the final stages. So yes, of course the crowd would be bitter, but the British do love an underdog – and Ivanišević certainly had claim to that.

In the end, it was the English weather that would provide the greatest upset in the semi-final, prolonging the agony of the British public for three days. Three. Whole. Days. The start of the match was as normal as it was going to get, given the occasion. Both players came out onto Centre Court as the cheering, roaring, applauding acoustics filled the goldfish bowl. The Union Jack flags were waved, jiggled and held high in the air as the players warmed up, optimism and excitement clinging tightly to every homemade poster and 'Go Tim' banner.

The chants from Henman Hill were equally euphoric and deafening; the SW19 version of Glastonbury in full voice. The first set didn't get off to a good start for anyone (aka 'everyone in Britain') wanting to see Tiger Tim get the first set under his belt. But after two hours of tennis, and despite Ivanišević securing the first set after playing some beautiful returns to secure the 12th game, Tim still looked distinctly champion-like.

He didn't let Ivanišević run away with the second set, instead holding his nerve to win a tense tie-break and take the second set 8-6. I say tense, but who doesn't like watching a tie-break? Especially when Henman had three break points in the second set and could have put us all out of our misery a bit sooner. But we digress. At one set all and playing some blistering volleys and tight-angled forehands that few believed he had in him, the Tiger roared in the third set. He ripped through Ivanišević's game like a predator on the attack and took the third set 6-0 in just 15 minutes. What was happening here? Was it a dream?

Tim maintained his momentum to take a 3-1 lead in the fourth set. Ivanišević, looking dejected and frustrated at the way the tables had turned, had no response to the succession of perfectly executed lobs Henman played. Oh my Lord, this was really happening. Tim looked like he could actually win!

But the British weather had something to say about that beacon of hope. As the rain started to fall and play was suspended until Saturday, the momentum for our Tim was broken. He appeared to lose his mojo overnight, and when the players came back onto Centre Court on Saturday, it was Ivanišević who looked like he had woken up from a bad dream and was about to set things right. In just 51 minutes of play before the rain put a halt to proceedings once again, the Croatian, having been 1-3 down, dug in his heels to take the third set to a tie-break.

Ivanišević's return of serve was brutal. Henman had no answer to the shots pummelled at his feet and he lost the fourth set. Our hero was down but not out. Now it was all to play for in the final set. But as each player held their serve, with Tim at 2-3 and 15-30, the rain started to fall once again and the semi-final was called to a halt once more. In just under an hour, the optimistic Centre Court crowd were crushed, and had to wait another gruelling night for the play to continue.

It did so at 1.15pm on the Sunday, but the rain break had once again renewed Ivanišević's sense of purpose and he broke Henman's serve – now lacking the attack of the second and third set – with pummelling returns. In true fighting spirit, Henman fought valiantly, soldiered on and very nearly brought the games level, but couldn't quite cut the mustard. Ivanišević had taken the lead and was serving at 5-3 for the match. And serve he did. Even two double faults weren't enough to stop him, and it was his 36th ace of the match that won him the semi-final.

Centre Court rose to cheer and commiserate with their fallen hero, and the appreciation for Ivanišević's gutsy tennis was clear. If our guy had to lose, then losing to someone who hadn't even been expected to make it past the first round was a bittersweet victory. At least, that is what we told ourselves.

Angela Mortimer vs Christine Truman

Date: 7 July 1961
Score: 4-6, 6-4, 7-5

*'I could hear the applause of the crowd but
not much else.'* Angela Mortimer

NOT SINCE 1914 (and never since this match) had Centre Court witnessed an all-British Ladies' final. The crowds that day weren't just treated to the certainty of a British champion, whatever the outcome, but they also enjoyed a match filled with drama and tension that made even those watching from the highest rims of Centre Court balance on the edge of their seats. This final had everything you could want; a player down but not out, dramatic injury, rain delays, a comeback from the underdog, and an epic conclusion that could have seen either player triumph.

The defending champion, Maria Bueno, did not make an appearance at this tournament due to ill health, and the top seed, Sandra Reynolds, was knocked out in the semi-final by Angela, 11-9, 6-3. As a side note, Sandra was the only South African player (male or female) to be seeded first in the opening of a Grand Slam singles event. Angela, the No. 7 seed, had reached the final before in 1958, an epic battle against reigning champion Althea Gibson, and was perhaps one of the most underrated British players in this post-war era.

But she didn't get off to the best of starts this time. Although she broke early on, it was clear that Christine was the crowd favourite; fans preferred her powerful serve and varied style of play over Angela's predictable baseline game. Christine came back from 3-1 down in the first set to gain control and put her stamp on proceedings. She was nine years younger than her opponent and, after her slow start, refused to let Angela into the game, taking control and the lead over her lower-seeded opponent. However, Angela had a fluid all-round game that had brought her this far, and she knew her own strengths and weaknesses. She was also partially deaf, which would be a difficult disability to overcome for many players, as she wasn't able to hear the sound of the ball coming off the strings, something that helps players to distinguish pace, power and placement of the ball. Angela had no such advantage, insisting instead that this quiet solitude was, in fact, its own benefit, as it allowed her to shut out all other distractions. After all, it certainly hadn't stopped her reaching the final of the Championships! At 29 years old, she also knew there might not be many more chances to lift the Wimbledon trophy, so this was an emotional final for her, one that favoured her steely and steady style of play. Her forehand drives and lobs were consistently played to a perfect length.

But just as the crowd were whipping out their umbrellas, the favourite, Christine, took the first set. As the rain grew heavier and the players left the court, many wondered whether this final would be over in a swiftly executed two sets. When the players emerged after a 40-minute break, the writing certainly seemed to be on the wall for Angela as Christine took the lead and looked set to break Angela's serve to go 5-3 up.

Things are rarely as predictable as they seem, however, and this was the point at which the game changed completely for both players. Trying to reach a shot that Angela had dropped over the net, Christine's quick change of direction caused her to fall. It wasn't an outrageous tumble, but it did give her cramp as she limped back to the baseline. The extent of this injury was unclear at first as the crowd applauded and encouraged her to continue to play. But it became clear very quickly that her movement was hindered, and Angela seized upon the heavy, slow reactions of her opponent to win the next five games and recover the second set.

It was now one set all and, for Angela, a tricky place to be. The crowd were favouring Christine, especially now that she was struggling on with injury, and yet it was Angela who played with a mind-over-matter attitude, having already come back from the brink to bring the match into a third set … Christine managed to play on and even stage a bit of a comeback herself, rediscovering her first-set form to level the third set at 5-5. It was another remarkable turnaround, and momentum was swinging from side to side as the crowd witnessed a fight to the bitter end.

Angela broke Christine's serve to go 6-5 up and serve for the match. With two Championship points to fend off, it proved too much for Christine. Her forehand found the net at 40-15, giving Angela the match. There was much clapping and admiration for both ladies as they acknowledged the crowd, the emotion of the occasion overwhelming for both winner and loser. Angela had done what she had set out to achieve; her persistence had paid off. She accepted the trophy from Princess Alice as Centre Court acknowledged their new British champion.

35

Andy Murray vs Novak Djokovic

Date: 7 July 2013
Score: 6-4, 7-5, 6-4

*'It makes his success even bigger because I
know the pressure and expectations he is
under. It is a great achievement. It was
an honour to be in this match, this final.'*
Novak Djokovic

I'M NOT sure there is anything you can write about a
match that is so one-sided in its hopes and dreams, so
filled with unbridled patriotic emotion, that you could
ever do it justice on paper. When all but a handful of the
15,000 spectators on Centre Court (the poster-waving,
face-painted, camera-holding, patriotic suit-wearing kind)
cheer for one player, when thousands of fans cram side by
side to watch his every move on the big screens around
the courts, and when millions of TV viewers shout loudly
without being heard by the one person they are cheering
for, there is no way to describe this game as anything

other than a celebration of one man making millions of dreams come true.

On the sunniest of Sundays the two men appeared on Centre Court, one of them carrying the hopes and dreams of several nations on his shoulders. This was the moment, as any and everybody liked to remind us, that we had been waiting 77 years to see; a British player crowned Wimbledon champion. Fred Perry, your work here is done. In just three hours and nine minutes (incidentally, there was a nine-hour queue to get into the grounds that morning) the nation watched Andy trundle his way through an encounter with the World No. 1, Novak Djokovic. Oh, how we will be harping about this for years to come. 'Do you remember where you were when ...?' and so forth. These things don't happen often. Let's make sure we put them in the memory bank and elaborate over time as the grandchildren ask us with incredulous intrigue.

The match itself wasn't a particularly dramatic or action-packed final, but that's beside the point. What Andy Murray did – in the stifling British summer heat – was still a world-class performance. Two double faults the whole match? That's a person who can control their nerves. Nine aces? That's a champ who can fire bullets when the going gets tough. That's our Andy. When he broke Djokovic's serve in the third game of the first set, it was with a beautifully timed, cleverly disguised backhand smash down the line – which, of course, got every single person watching excited. After an hour of play – in on-court temperatures recorded at 49°C and with barely a waft of breeze – Andy took the first set.

If Djokovic was frustrated with his 17 unforced errors in that maiden set, it showed. He was now striking every ball with a ferocity that had been lacking and he was in full swing. He took a 4-1 lead in the second set and, after an hour and a half on court, was firing on all cylinders. Our Andy was sweating and hiding in his towel between games, but just as quickly as his attack seemed to slow down, his mojo returned (with a little help from a cap to keep the sun out of his eyes), and when Djokovic double-faulted at the end of the seventh game, Andy brought the scores back level.

At 5-5, and with Djokovic serving at 15-all, it all got a bit explosive. Believing that a baseline shot Murray had sent to Djokovic's feet was out – but with no line call given and no challenges left – the otherwise mild-mannered No. 1 seed got angry. And he got angrier still when he smashed a forehand into the net, allowing Murray to serve for the second set. And he turned into Mr Angry of Angryville when Murray aced him to do just that.

And so to the third set, which no one really believed would be the last of the match, but those of a nervous disposition were certainly grateful that it was. And talk about a belter of a start for our hero, as he broke Djokovic in the first game and took a 2-0 lead. Oh, but silly us. We were getting ahead of ourselves and Djokovic quite rightly put us back in our place. He broke back, held, broke back again and held again. Our hero was now 2-4 down. But whatever Djokovic could do, handy Andy could do better. With an almighty explosion of jaw-dropping forehand drives, Murray brought the scores back level before breaking Djokovic at 4-4.

'Steady, Andy, steady …' thought the hearts and minds of the nation. It was 5.10pm. Andy was serving for the Championship now. Surely, this has to be it. He raced to 40-0 and the whole country was aware that he had three lives, three chances, three Championship points … but he let all three points slip away! But when he secured advantage after saving a break point from Djokovic, he earned himself a fourth chance. It was time. A 130mph serve, a frantic return, a pummelling forehand and then a final shot from Djokovic into the net. The nations rejoiced. Andy fell to his knees in triumph and there wasn't a dry eye in the house. And when he clambered up to the players' box to hug, kiss and celebrate with his mum and coaching team, this pregnant, hormonal and emotional writer sobbed like a trooper in front of her bewildered toddler. It's these moments that are etched forever, not just in your mind's recollection, but in the memories of your heart.

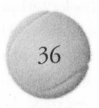

36

Serena Williams vs Heather Watson

Date: 4 July 2015
Score: 6-2, 4-6, 7-5

*'I was super, super close. I think that's what
hurts the most.'* Heather Watson

THIS WAS a third-round match many believed would be
a box-ticking exercise for former Wimbledon champion
Serena Williams as she embarked on another charge for
the Ladies' Singles crown. But how wrong they were.
How wrong we all were! If the Centre Court spectators
suspected they might be the driving force behind one of
the biggest upsets in the Championships that year, they
were using it to their full advantage. Never had a crowd of
cheering, shouting, flag-waving fans been more vocal in a
third-round game than they were in the sunshine of 2015,
as Serena and British hopeful Heather Watson came out
onto court. This was a momentous occasion for Heather.
The British No. 1 had never faced the mighty Serena
before. This was her idol, the player she had on her posters

adorning her bedroom walls when she was growing up, and now here Serena was, the five-time Wimbledon champion, stepping out next to her on Centre Court. If this was a 'pinch me' moment for Heather, it was only going to get a lot more remarkable.

The last time Heather reached the third round, she had been thrashed 6-0, 6-2 by Agnieszka Radwańska and admitted afterwards that she tried too hard, too soon. Her approach this year was to remember that everyone is human and that therefore everyone, even the World No. 1, is beatable. The moment the players came out, the decibel level doubled. One spectator walking to an outside court thought that Heather had actually won the match, given the cacophony of cheers emitting from Centre Court. Oh, if only.

But there was little doubt that the crowd were on the British hopeful's side, with chants of 'If you love Heather Watson, clap your hands' reverberating around Centre Court. It had been a long time since there'd been a British Ladies' Wimbledon champion and the crowd sensed they could help to cause an upset if they continued to support their home player. Not that Serena was in any mood to mess around. That was clear from the warm-up, when she nearly smacked a ball into a line judge's head. Furious? Yes, and getting a little peeved with the crowd, it seemed.

With two aces in the first game, Serena won her serve. But Heather replied with an ace of her own and, although it took a little longer to close out the game, she drew the match level. Of course, the cheers were deafening and horrifically exaggerated, given the score was only 1-1 and there was a long way to go. Serena showed the crowd and critics what she was made of to win the next two games, breaking Heather to go 4-1 up, but Heather remained undeterred and, with a blistering backhand down the line, secured her service game.

Serena's serves proved too much for Heather and the top seed won her next game before breaking Heather in the final game of the set. It did little to quieten the crowd, although some spectators, believing they had been given a reality check, fell back on the British reserve of the stiff upper lip instead. The press box abandoned their seats to start writing a polite, if predictable, piece reporting on another Serena win and another British hopeful crashing out. But they had failed to give Heather credit. She was down, but a long way from out.

At one set down and holding her serve to go 1-1 in the second, every point Heather played and won was met by resounding cheers from the Centre Court crowd. Henman Hill exploded in appreciative claps and cheers as the action played out on screen, and Wimbledon's grounds came alive in response to the action that was taking place just a few days into the Championships. Holding her serve again to go 2-2, what happened next certainly made things interesting. Either it happened because of a lapse in concentration or perhaps frustration at the baying crowd, but, at break point, Serena missed her first serve and then sent her second into the net. The unthinkable had just happened.

Serena regained composure and broke Heather back, but our plucky underdog refused to fold and, at 4-4, an exasperated Serena produced some wildly erratic shots and was broken again. Heather now faced the opportunity to serve for the second set and many would forgive the British No. 1 for feeling the pressure. Yet she didn't and she did indeed take the second set, causing an uproar within Centre Court. Could you imagine what would happen if she reached the final?! OK, we were way ahead of ourselves.

Heather had found an inner strength and forced Serena into a third set. The decider was on and the crowd couldn't believe the turn the match had taken. Twitter went berserk with commentators and sports stars commanding everyone to stop what they were doing and tune into the deciding set of what had become an unbelievable match. To top off the tension, excitement and the cries of 'could this be one of the greatest days in British tennis history?' Heather broke Serena in the third set. And then won her serve. Could this really be true? With Serena looking like a defeated woman, her head hung low, the crowd added insult to injury by cheering every missed point she made.

Now, given that she was a respected Wimbledon champion, this sort of heckling was something of a new occurrence for Serena and she wasn't pleased. She was agitated. And the boos when she scored a point didn't help either. Heather had a 3-0 lead over the player she had admired since she was a young girl and was, whisper it, looking like she could cause one of the greatest Wimbledon upsets of all time. Serena is famously quoted as saying: '… a champion is defined not by their wins but by how they can recover when they fall.' She might be down, but she was certainly not out. In fact, she won the next three games to level the set.

At 4-4, Heather turned to the crowd and encouraged the volume to be turned up a notch. And they obliged tenfold. Serena then lost her service game, leaving Heather to serve for the match. This was not for the faint-hearted and, sadly, it was not to be. But oh so close! There was a collective holding of heads on Murray Mound as Heather crashed out after putting up such an incredible fight, and the standing ovation was testament to the bravery she showed throughout the two hours 15 minutes of action on court. One day, one day …

'What's the toughest away match to play?' Serena was asked afterwards. 'A French player at Roland Garros? An Australian at the Rod Laver Arena?' Unsurprisingly, it didn't take her long to answer. 'I'm going to have to go with playing Heather Watson in Great Britain, for sure.'

37

Steffi Graf vs Monica Seles

Date: 4 July 1992
Score: 6-2, 6-1

*'Even if I do keep grunting, I just feel
it shouldn't have been such a big issue
pointed out to me the whole two weeks.'*
Monica Seles

SILENCE MIGHT be golden, but chances are that
Monica Seles would have something to say about that.
After two weeks of coverage and negative press about the
noise she made when striking a ball, she decided to play
the final of the Ladies' Singles that year in utter silence.
Grunting was her thing, it was part of her game, and –
until the two weeks of Wimbledon – there had been no
implication that anything was wrong with her 'grunts'
when she won in Australia and then at the French Open
(where she beat Steffi 6-2, 3-6, 10-8).

But at Wimbledon it was a very real problem. In her
semi-final against Martina Navratilova, which she won

6-2, 6-7, 6-4, Monica was given two warnings by the umpire after Martina complained that she couldn't hear the ball. Interestingly, however, it wasn't until she had lost the first set that she lodged the complaint. The quarter-final before that also brought with it a lot of 'Shrieking Seles' headlines when her opponent, Nathalie Tauziat, also complained to the umpire.

The British media seized on all of this attention, dubbing her 'Moaning Monica'. A gruntometer was used by the British tabloids to record the decibel levels of the young star. So you can forgive Monica for being a bit quiet when it came to the final, not wanting to take any of the shine off the momentous occasion and her hopes of achieving a Grand Slam if she continued on her path to victory.

However, as well as the British press, there is one other element that keeps the top players on their toes at Wimbledon – the weather. On one of the most frustratingly wet Saturdays ever, Steffi and Monica were subjected to three rain delays, totalling four hours and 24 minutes of waiting and contemplating. Steffi was chasing her fourth Wimbledon title and the chance to prove she might be able to reclaim her No. 1 ranking, which she had lost to Monica the previous year.

If the crowd were expecting a dramatic final, they would be disappointed. And wet. The match lasted just 58 minutes in total, but for Monica it probably felt a lot longer. Steffi came out firing on all cylinders and didn't let Monica find her rhythm (or voice) in the first set. Even though Monica had two break points in the seventh game at 2-4 (which was the longest game of the match, producing four deuces), it was Steffi's killer forehand shots that were too much for a struggling Monica.

But the score doesn't always reflect the action. Monica showed off a few new shots, slicing the ball more, hitting a few big serves and not being afraid to take a few risks. But then she had to; Steffi's court coverage was phenomenal. When she broke Monica to reach set point, she was clearly showing who was dominating the game. Monica's 47 unforced errors also contributed to the near whitewash victory for Steffi. Monica was struggling with her serves and double faults and played as if she would prefer to be anywhere else in the world apart from a drizzly grass court in the Wimbledon final. Surely there is nowhere else in the world?!

As the rain clouds gathered, the first rain delay came after Steffi had won the first set and taken a 1-0 lead in the second. The players came back onto court after a 46-minute wait, with Monica hoping to hold her service game and get back into the set. The 18-year-old came out looking a lot more relaxed after the first delay, while commentators speculated whether the grunt might come back after a chat with her coach, perhaps in a bid to make her play more aggressively and less defensively, a style of play that we had been used to seeing. This was an important game for Monica. She needed to hold her serve and reassert her authority in the second set. But the rain had other ideas and the umbrellas came back out with the score tied at deuce as the players went back into the changing rooms.

With a rain delay of 90 minutes, the players had chance to read their fan mail and rest, but the frustration must have got to Monica. While rain delays often favour the player behind, for Monica this wasn't the case. She did manage to hold her serve to equal the set at 1-1, but she couldn't seem to settle into the match again. Steffi continued to dictate the action and ran down more balls, while Monica continued to be outplayed. She couldn't break Steffi or even win another game.

Steffi served for the Championship and, at 40-15, won the final point with an ace. It was a golden touch for an otherwise grey day. This was the only Wimbledon final Monica contested during her career. She came close again in 1998, 2000 and 2002, but lost in the quarter-final each time. Whether it was a shriek that gave her a spark, we'll never know. Only that on that very dismal and wet final, Monica's spirit was definitely dampened.

38

Lori McNeil vs Steffi Graf

Date: 21 June 1994
Score: 7-5, 7-6

'She was better than me, that was obvious.'
Steffi Graf

AS WITH any other major tournament, big upsets happen at Wimbledon. But no upset drew a greater gasp than defending champion Steffi Graf's first-round defeat in the competition. Wimbledon had barely had time to pour an extra portion of cream on its strawberries before the five-time winner of the Championship (1988, 1989, 1991, 1992, 1993) was eliminated by the unseeded American player, Lori McNeil. If you didn't know her name before this match, you certainly did afterwards.

If the 30-year-old was intimidated by the occasion, she didn't show it. Her strategy was to play her serve-and-volley game and exploit Steffi's weaker backhand. Most opponents didn't ever get the chance to execute their own attack against the top seed, but the spark was missing in Steffi this year, causing her to lose control of the game.

The rain provided the backdrop to the occasion as play was interrupted for nearly three hours. This wasn't an unusual occurrence, nor was it expected to cause any major issue – especially for Steffi, who had been winning Wimbledon titles in wet conditions since she first upset Martina Navratilova in 1988. She was used to breaking records, but this wasn't one she – or anyone in the crowd that gloomy day – saw coming. She was to become the first reigning champion in the tournament's history to be knocked out in the first round.

To say Steffi lost rather than Lori won would be incredibly unfair to the American, as her style of play was polished and attacking. She owned the grass court that day, looking like she had been playing in finals for years, and going up against a formidable opponent clearly wasn't a nerve-racking experience for her. In contrast, Steffi was unnerved and lacked concentration from the off. It was the sort of display not many had witnessed from her in her career, and while her strength of character often allowed her to be down in the first set and come back to win matches, something in her determination failed that day on Centre Court and she never recovered from a first-set drubbing.

'I am shocked,' confirmed one drenched spectator, who had been waiting to watch her favourite player begin her Wimbledon journey to the final. 'I came here expecting to see more of Steffi over the next two weeks and now that she's going home, I'm going home!'

Lori's victory over Steffi came down to a few factors. Although unseeded, she was at home on the grass courts and, more importantly, could bring her skills to the surface. She had come fresh from a victory at Edgbaston, winning the singles title in the run-up to Wimbledon, and had honed her grass game with 1990 Wimbledon finalist, Zina Garrison. She had beaten Steffi once before, two years previously, in the opening round of the WTA Tour Championships. This set the scene for a good match, but there was nothing Steffi's fans needed to be too concerned about.

Murmurs of an upset started to spread around Centre Court when Lori broke Steffi in the first set to take a 2-0 lead. The blustery conditions made play unusually awkward for a June day, but not unplayable. When the first drops of rain began to fall after Lori had made another three service breaks, the action was tied at 5-5 and it was time for a break. And, many assumed, a chance for the reigning champion to regroup and refocus. They had only been playing for 38 minutes, but the rain stoppage seemed like the ideal opportunity for Steffi to regain her composure.

After nearly one hour and 30 minutes the players returned to court, with Lori enthused and primed to continue her attack. With serves that played to Steffi's backhand – deep enough to deny her the chance to switch and change to a forehand return – meant that Lori held her service game to go 6-5. If the crowd were expecting Steffi to launch a similar attack in her service game, they were wrong. Lori won the first set when Steffi doubled-faulted on the second set point, hitting her first serve long and finding the net with the second. It was after the second rain delay, this time one hour and 43 minutes, that the crowd saw the old Steffi back on court, taking control of the second set and creating a set point at 5-3.

It was now 6.20pm and, far from being a glorious summer evening, the rain clouds still loomed overhead and threatened to disrupt play once again. But they didn't need to. Lori served an ace to save the set point that would perhaps have signalled a change in fortunes in the match, and she went on to draw the games level at 5-5. In the tie-break, two costly mistakes by Steffi – a smash from close range that found the net and a double fault – gave Lori a lead. And it was a confidently struck backhand volley that won her the shootout in the end, and with it the match.

The two lengthy rain delays meant that the match took place across five hours, but Lori's swift execution of Steffi played out in just one hour and 43 minutes.

Head hung low, a defeated Steffi walked off Centre Court and straight to the airport, wanting to put this year's Championships behind her. Meanwhile Lori advanced to the semi-final stage, battling it out and eventually losing to Conchita Martínez 3-6, 6-2, 10-8. She never advanced past the third round of a Grand Slam tournament again, and her singles career ended in 1999. Steffi regained her composure to come back to Wimbledon the following year and win back her crown. She also won it the year after that. In 1995, when she won the US Open, she became the only woman in history to win each of the four Grand Slam titles at least four times. The champion might have been down in 1994, but she most definitely wasn't out.

Rafael Nadal vs Roger Federer

Date: 6 July 2008
Score: 6-4, 6-4, 6-7, 6-7, 9-7

'I believe the rain delay probably woke me up. I said, "If you are going to go out of this match, at least you're going to go down swinging."' Roger Federer

CELEBRITY-FILLED CROWD? Check. Mood lighting? Check. Rain to add suspense? Check. Two of the world's best tennis players ready to meet in the final for the third year running? Check, check. If you were setting the scene for the most majestic and thrilling sporting final to take place on a small patch of grass, in a small borough of London, you would be hard pushed to match the 2008 final between these two titans. No. 2 seed Nadal was hoping to dethrone the Swiss King, who was making claim to a sixth title. Would his five-year reign be coming to an end? Could the crowd bear to watch? Would Federer be able to see the ball? Like all good stories, let's start at the beginning …

The Fedal bromance slash rivalry had begun two years previously, when the pair met in the All England Club's Men's Singles final, with Federer looking for a new playmate after Andy Roddick, his previous final buddy, had been knocked out in the third round. Enter the young bandana-wearing Spanish bull, who had the guts to take on the Swiss cheese, but didn't get the glory. The sequel came in the following year, but we all know sequels are never as good, unless you are McEnroe and Borg – see Match 5. And so we find ourselves at the final instalment of the trilogy, setting the scene on one of the world's biggest sporting stages, where there is no rehearsal time and no hiding place as 15,000 sets of eyes follow your every move. The theatre was due for renovation – the all-new sparkling roof was going to be installed ready for the following year's tournament – so this was the last year the rain and darkness would interfere in a final.

As the players walked out onto that imposing stage, 35 minutes later than originally planned due to the rain, the play in the very first point of the match was a good indication of how the rest of the final was going to pan out. It was a 14-stroke rally that saw both men show their speed and agility around the court until Nadal smashed a forehand straight down the line. With such a fiercely contested first point, the crowd knew they were in for the long haul. When Nadal broke first, in the third game of the set, he had laid down the challenge to the reigning champion ... this is my turf now.

He went on to win the first set, narrowly escaping two break-point opportunities from the monarch to take it 6-4. Expectations for set two were high; no one in the crowd dared blink for fear of missing out on a single shot. Federer broke serve early in the second set in a charging attack that saw him go 4-1 ahead. He had taken the lead but not yet the set. Nadal came galloping forth, winning the next five games in a row to take the second set from under Federer's nose.

As the dark clouds started to appear overhead, Nadal was fired up for the third set. He knew that Federer had come back from the jaws of defeat before and that there would be no chance to relax until the final shot had been played. There was a sense that Federer wasn't anywhere near finished; we just had to wait and see when the comeback would emerge ...

At 3-3 in the third set, Federer was down 0-40 and a crucial break for Nadal looked very much on the cards. Federer won the next five points in a row and, at 4.51pm as the rain made its entrance (boo, hiss), he was leading 5-4.

The hour's rain delay gave both stars an opportunity to regroup and, as play resumed at 6.11pm, anticipation was high for the continuation of play. And continue it did! The third set went to a tie-break, with Federer's mammoth serve acing his opponent and the roar of the crowd taking him to a set victory.

The fourth set was tight. Both held serve until, suddenly, Federer was serving to stay in the match at 4-5 and 0-30. The twitchiness grew amongst the fans chanting 'Roger! Roger!' on repeat. He stayed calm, held his nerve, and another tie-break was about to start.

Nadal was up 5-2 and had two serves to go, but tension proved to be his downfall (in real terms, a double fault and then a shot into the net) and he let his first Championship point slip off his strings ... Federer missed the chance to take the set with a mishit, and then Nadal earned another Championship point at 7-6, but the King's serve was again too strong. At 7-7, Nadal played a baseline shot that left the crowd and the reigning champion open-mouthed and, once again, he was serving for the Championship. This time it was a Federer return, a backhand that showed no sign of nerves, hurtling past the open-mouthed Spaniard. Federer took the next two points and the fourth set. You couldn't make this up.

Now this was the big one. The decider. The final set. History told us that five-time champion Federer, who had come back from two sets down, would surely have confidence and momentum in his corner. The hopeless thrill seeker in us felt there would still be more to come from Nadal. And so there was. But not before the rain came again. It was just before 8pm. When the players returned after a half-hour delay, the feeling around Centre Court was that this would surely go into a second day; there was a maximum of 60 minutes' light remaining and no one was expecting the fifth set to be a slapdash affair.

And so the drama began. It was a beautiful, mesmerising, jaw-dropping display of tennis from two of the greats, every ounce of their beings going into every shot, and there was no let-up from either player. At 5-5, Nadal had two break points flung back in his face as Federer held from 15-40. Then as the minute hand swept past 9pm, with the scores tied at 7-7, the light was the only dull thing about this unbelievable final. In the dusky, dim light the organisers knew they would have to allow two more games to be played, so that both players had the chance to come back the next day level.

In the end, only two more games were needed to see a new champion emerge from the darkness. Federer was unable to hold all four break points against him, and Nadal, after changing ends, was now serving for the title. Centre Court had never been so still, so silent. At 40-30, on Championship point, Nadal fired a bullet serve at Federer and everyone held their breath, but Federer's champion instinct pulled out a magical backhand drive that dipped as it flew past Nadal. This was going to be the last game of the day, whatever happened next. But as it happened, it was Federer's last point of this epic final. An unreturnable serve took Nadal to another Championship point, and then Federer's forehand return found the net. Nadal fell to the floor in disbelief as the Centre Court crowd took the roof off and the darkness finally fell. The flashing of the press light bulbs reflected off the golden trophy, illuminating the new champion of Wimbledon.

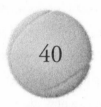

40

Martina Navratilova and Pam Shriver vs Kathy Jordan and Anne Smith

Date: 4 July 1981
Score: 6-3, 7-6

'Martina's the greatest female tennis player there has ever been. But even she couldn't win a doubles tournament on her own. I played my part.' Pam Shriver

IN 1981, Navratilova was top dog, firmly positioning herself as the World No. 1 in the singles game and enjoying her time at the top. She could have been forgiven if she wanted to concentrate on her singles game and continue to notch up those titles, but for Martina, playing doubles was a big advantage – it gave her extra practice time and more competition experience. There was no doubting that when it came to playing doubles, Navratilova's intensity and competitive spirit were as high as they were in her singles games, and any partner would have to match her energy and drive if she wanted to stay on her side. Enter Pam Shriver.

Pam was playing in a tournament in Florida in October 1980 when she received a phone call from Navratilova. It probably took all of a few minutes before Shriver agreed to Martina's request to join forces as a doubles pairing. They had met on the singles circuit 40 times previously, with Shriver winning just three of those games, so the old adage 'if you can't beat 'em, join 'em' must have been ringing in her ears. They lost in their first ever match, but by the time they played in their first major tournament the kinks had been ironed out.

And so we come to Wimbledon in 1981. This match makes the cut for two reasons. Firstly, it was the first Grand Slam title win for Shriver, and secondly, it marked the beginning of one of the most formidable partnerships the tennis world has ever seen. Navratilova was no stranger to Grand Slam victories, having already won three singles titles (including two at Wimbledon). She was unstoppable on court and now, teaming up with Shriver, the pair set the doubles world alight.

Shriver fell at the semi-final stage in the Singles competition that year, losing out in an emotional match to Chris Evert, who went on to win the Singles title. Like Navratilova, Shriver was a natural serve-and-volley player – perhaps one of the main reasons they won so effortlessly. During the 1981 final on Centre Court, the couple knew they had to get to the net to survive, and they did just that. Not only did they survive, but the crowd bore witness to the beginnings of this magical pairing that would go on to conquer the ladies' doubles circuit for the next decade.

If fans enjoyed watching Navratilova in action on the singles court, there was even more to enjoy when she played doubles, as this final clearly showed. When Martina served, she adjusted her speed so that both Jordan and Smith found it tricky to return her formidable left-handed strike. When Shriver stayed at the baseline, she knew Martina had the middle of the court covered, and both had quick reflexes, making it hard for either Jordan or Smith to find a way around or over. In the end, it was the low and consistent power returns that gave them an edge. Rarely had opponents been faced with such overwhelming power, and Martina's high forehand volleys were best left well alone!

Shriver made sure she played her part, winning many points against the defending champions with her fierce cross-court forehands and sharp volleys. Pam's strong play, together with the athleticism and power of Navratilova, meant that the final at the All England Club was always going to go the way of the new dynamic duo. Jumping for joy as the winning shot was played, Martina and Pam were every bit as ecstatic as the cheering crowd, knowing their incredible partnership was cause for celebration. And so it proved. Their record-breaking span of 109 consecutive wins from April 1983 to July 1985, when they were beaten in the Wimbledon final by Kathy Jordan and Liz Smylie, remains unbeaten. When they split up in 1989, they had won 74 titles together, 20 in major tournaments and five titles at SW19. But for the lucky spectators who were watching that day in 1981, this was the start of the dream team's dominance.

Novak Djokovic vs Roger Federer

Date: 14 July 2019
Score: 7-6, 1-6, 7-6, 4-6, 13-12

'That was a crazy match, it was long, it had everything. Novak, congratulations man, that was crazy.' Roger Federer

IF YOU'VE ever thought, 'I'll wait and have a cuppa once the match is over,' while you're watching the action from SW19 at home, you're making a rookie mistake. Unless you have someone willing to get up and make a brew midway through a final (you'd probably have to bribe them), chances are that the kettle will remain unboiled for a good couple of hours. In the case of this final, nearly five hours. All this talk of tea is not purely out of a sense of Britishness (tea and scones, anyone?), but because we weren't alone in our thirst-quenching routines. The national grid reported a surge in power after the final shot had been played in the Djokovic/Federer final. No one had dared move for four hours and 57 minutes and it made history as the longest Men's final ever at Wimbledon. Incidentally, the previous record also featured Federer, in 2008, when he lost out to Rafael Nadal.

No. 1 seed Djokovic was hoping for his fifth title, while No. 2 seed Federer was aiming for his ninth. It was a match between two masters of their art, two athletes in a class of their own. Djokovic took the first set in a tie-break that saw him win four straight points. It was a sign of things to come, each point being fought with valour.

And yet the second set saw eight-time champion Federer blast his opponent out of the water to level the match. Perhaps it was a slight drop-off in Djokovic's intensity that saw Federer barrel through the first three games and then keep barrelling to a 6-1 set win.

The third set saw another tie-break go in favour of Djokovic, another battle of wills and destructive shots, although he did almost blow a 5-1 lead. He now only needed the fourth set to win it, but Federer had other ideas – it wasn't over until the older guy said it was over! And he certainly wasn't done yet. With a two-break lead, Federer managed to hold his nerve and clinch the fourth set, bringing the scores level. To say this was an even match in terms of support would be a big fat lie. One or two in the crowd were shouting for the Serbian, but they were drowned out by cheers for the man who had given Wimbledon so many exciting and tantalising finals over the years.

It was all down to the fifth set. And it was a fifth set that lasted more than two hours. The 'Roger! Roger!' chants were deafening, as were the unsporting cheers when Djokovic made the occasional error or double fault. In contrast, groans reverberated around Centre Court whenever Federer made an error, followed by rousing and continued shouts of encouragement. Roger had the heart and soul of the home crowd wrapped around his racket, and played with the spirit of a man who knew that his days of playing in finals on this great stage might perhaps – just perhaps – be numbered. Not that we wanted to think about that, of course. For now, he was charging around the court like he did when he won his first title 16 years previously.

Interestingly, Djokovic had a selective-hearing plan prepared as he entered Centre Court, knowing that it was unlikely he would hear anything above the roar of Federer fans. 'I like to transmute it in a way: when the crowd is chanting "Roger!" I hear "Novak!" I try to convince myself that it's like that.'*

At 8-7 in the final set, Federer had two match points on his serve when an ace gave him a 40-15 lead. If Djokovic felt the pressure, he didn't show it. Both match points were saved by the defending champion. Federer had faltered. Djokovic wasn't going to let him get that close again and brought the game back to deuce before breaking back. Hearts were breaking, nerves were shattering, cushions were being thrown/hidden behind/ cuddled as the rollercoaster of emotions hit the millions of viewers watching at home. And still no cup of tea.

At 12 games all, the new rules for a fifth-set tie-break came into play. Previously, players would fight out the final set until the bitter end, but this year, for the first time, if the games reached 12 all there would be a tie-break. The All England Club chairman, Philip Brook, announced the changes in October the previous year, stating that the new scoring system would ensure matches 'reach a conclusion in an acceptable time frame'. Or perhaps he still had the Isner/Mahut match fresh in his mind and didn't want anyone to die of exhaustion on his watch (see Match 47).

Djokovic had won the previous two tie-breaks in the match. Would he win the third and decisive one? After four hours and 48 minutes of play, we were about to see which Wimbledon champion had the fight left in them. Djokovic's forehand proved mightier when it mattered most and, after Djokovic challenged a ball that was called out, Hawk-Eye revealed that the point would indeed need to be replayed. And the replayed point was the point that mattered. When the ball found Federer's racket frame rather than his strings, the game was all over.

The heartbroken crowd took some solace from the numbers behind the game. Their guy had won more points on his first serve, had powered 25 aces compared to Djokovic's ten, had hit fewer double faults, had won a greater percentage of points behind his first serve, second serve and net points, had converted more break points and had hit 94 winners to Djokovic's 54. But if we were looking at numbers, the most important was matches won that day: Djokovic 1 Federer 0. Plus, Djokovic was the first man in the Open Era to save Championship points in a final and go on to win. Tennis could be a cruel game, but what a beautifully played game it was to watch. And *now* it was time for a well-earned cup of tea. And if there was one solace, it seemed that Roger had no plans to retire just yet, giving everyone everywhere (including Djokovic) optimism that age really is just a number when it comes to playing world-class tennis.

'Roger said he hopes it gives other people hope they can do this at 37,' admitted the new champion. 'I'm one of them.'

*This also works for us ... we only hear positive and raving reviews if any criticism is volleyed around.

42

John Austin and Tracy Austin vs Dianne Fromholtz and Mark Edmondson

Date: 5 July 1980
Score: 4-6, 7-6, 6-3

*'Don't panic? That's the dumbest thing I've
ever heard in my life.'* Tracy Austin

BEFORE VENUS and Serena Williams flew the flag
for siblings teaming up to take over the world, American
brother and sister combo, John and Tracy Austin, made
history by winning the Mixed Doubles title in 1980. It
perhaps wasn't too surprising if you knew the Austin
family, though; they had tennis balls in their genes. Their
other siblings – brother Jeff and sister Pam – were both
touring professionals and, with Tracy appearing on the
front cover of *World Tennis* magazine at just four years
old, this sort of historical accolade could well have been
foretold.

Tracy went to Wimbledon for the first time as a fresh-
faced 16-year-old in 1979, battling through to the semi-

final, where she faced one of her childhood heroes, Billie Jean King. Billie had visited the tennis club Tracy played at when she was in fourth grade, igniting a spark in the young Austin, and a desire to one day become World No. 1 herself. She didn't have to wait long. She beat Billie 6-4, 6-7, 6-2 before losing out 7-5, 6-1 to Martina Navratilova in the final. But this taste of near victory spurred her on to produce some outstanding tennis for someone so young. She beat Chris Evert in the US Open final in straight sets later that year. She is still the youngest champion in US Open history, winning the title at 16 years and eight months old.

When she arrived at the All England Club the following year in 1980, she was ranked No. 2 in the world. Commentators predicted that she could be lifting the Venus Rosewater Dish if she continued to upset the big names in the way she had been doing. As well as competing in the Ladies' Singles that year, she had also teamed up with big brother to start their journey as a pairing in the Mixed Doubles, advancing through the rounds with relative ease. The siblings entered the competition unseeded, but managed to beat No. 3 seeds and formidable Australian duo, John Newcombe and Evonne Goolagong, 2-6, 7-6, 6-4 in the second round.

They then beat their third-round opponents in straight sets. With a heightened sense of confidence, they then took out their quarter-final opponents, Colin Dowdeswell and Greer Stevens, in straight sets, 7-6, 6-1. Meanwhile Tracy had made it through to the semi-final in the Singles competition and, in a hard-fought battle, eventually lost to Evonne Goolagong. Her agent tried to persuade her to head back to the States and rest before the US Open, but going home now would leave John without a partner and she wasn't about to let big bro down. Besides, perhaps there was still one trophy within reach that might have the Austin name engraved on it that year.

It turned out to be a good decision. The Austins faced the No. 1 seeds, Betty Stöve and Frew McMillan, in the semi-final. Most were predicting that this would be the end of the brother/sister journey in the Mixed Doubles event. But the Austins had other ideas. They were in it to win it and they wanted to make history. Tracy's two-handed backhand was reliable, her net game solid, and she served a high percentage of first serves (which didn't set any records for speed or power), meaning that she rarely double-faulted on grass. John, who only reached No. 40 in the world rankings during his professional career, had a strong passing shot and a dominant baseline drive. Not only did they beat the top seeds, they beat them convincingly, winning 6-4, 6-2.

With that win under their belt, they now had to face another Aussie tandem, Dianne Fromholtz and Mark Edmondson, in the final. This match didn't quite get off to the same positive start and, for the first time in the tournament, the siblings weren't playing in sync. Or playing well at all, for that matter. With Mama and Papa Austin watching on from the players' box, they lost the first set and went 4-1 down in the second.

Deciding that his sister needed some form of encouragement, John tried to tell her to calm down and 'don't panic' in the break before the sixth game of that set. 'That's the dumbest thing I've ever heard in my life,' came Tracy's response. We're not sure if that's true, but whether it was or not, it was the start of the Austin comeback. They turned the game around and forced a third set. The tightness had gone from their game, as had Tracy's agitation towards her brother for trying to offer relaxation advice. They played with the composed, natural style they had displayed previously in the tournament.

They cruised to victory in that final set, with John serving for the match and securing that all-important sixth game. The pair lifted their hands in celebration before John lifted up his little sister in an extra show of triumph as the first brother and sister to ever achieve such a feat. Perhaps spurred on by his encouraging words that seemed to inject the spark back into his sister's game, John eventually retired from professional tennis and focused more on coaching, teaching the likes of Pete Sampras, Robbie Weiss and Michael Chang, to name a few. Perhaps his words weren't so dumb after all.

43

Betty Stöve vs Sue Barker

Date: 30 June 1977
Score: 6-4, 2-6, 6-4

*'I just played a really horrible match from
start to finish, I can't be any more blunt
than that. And I was bitterly, bitterly
disappointed. I let the whole side down.'*
Sue Barker

IT WAS 1977, the year Virginia Wade won the Ladies'
Singles title in the Queen's Silver Jubilee year. But how
different that Wimbledon final might have been, eh? In
a match that never was, Sue Barker was favourite to win
the head-to-head with Virginia, having beaten her three
out of the four times they had met that year. The cover
of the *Radio Times* carried a picture of Sue clutching
her tennis racket and featured the headline 'Sue courts
success', accompanied by the line, 'Sue Barker is our big
hope for the Women's Singles.' But the big hope never
quite made it. Sue lost out in the semi-final to the Dutch

player she thought she would easily beat. She admitted years later that the thought of playing Virginia in the final meant that she didn't concentrate fully on her semi-final game first. It wasn't even a rookie mistake; Sue had won the French Open the previous year, beating Czech player Renáta Tomanová, who had been a finalist in the Australian Open.

In the Silver Jubilee year, the excitement and buzz around the women's game was at an all-time high, and the talk from commentators, media and fans alike was that an all-British Ladies' final might be on the cards. Sue, No. 4 seed, versus Virginia Wade, No. 3 seed. Chris Evert was the defending champion, but had been beaten by Virginia in the semi-final. Now all Sue had to do in order to give the British public the final they craved was to do the same and win her semi-final.

Her opponent, No. 7 seed Betty Stöve, was beatable and, as they came out onto Centre Court, the sun was shining and the crowd were cheering. The entire nation was hopeful. Sue didn't get off to the rosiest of starts, but she was forgiven and cheered on by the crowd, who were repeatedly asked to stay quiet during the rallies. As if! When Sue took the second set, at the second time of asking, it looked like the predictions might come true after all. Was an all-British Ladies' final looming?

Sue and Betty had been playing for just over an hour, and now all Sue had to do was hold her nerve. She was playing well, her forehand was strong and she was able to move Betty around the court easily. When she broke Betty in the first game to go 1-0 in the final set, it was the perfect start she needed. But then she lost her service game, mostly due to double faults, and suddenly the home player didn't seem to have such a strong advantage. She still had the crowd, however, and although Sue felt the pressure of Betty's serve, she knew her own was just as strong if she didn't add extra tension to it. Sue also knew how dangerous Betty was at the net and tried to keep her back at her baseline as much as she could. At two games all, Betty began to launch an attack that Sue couldn't quite keep up with. But that's not to say Betty's game was unbeatable. That is the problem with this semi-final, however you see it. Betty was entirely beatable but seemed the more relaxed player, while Sue was becoming increasingly frustrated.

Things looked bleak for Sue when Betty took the lead to 5-2, but she wasn't going to give in – not with that crowd. Even with a frustrating line call, Sue managed to hold her serve and then do the unthinkable – she broke back. It was Betty's turn to look a little shaky on her serves. With the crowd cheering her every point, Sue found a forehand return that just skimmed the net and dropped over – a sign of good fortune – to give her break point on Betty's service game. It was a game that showed true grit and Sue even saved match point when Betty's high volley went wide. The tension was incredible, but when Sue finally broke to bring the match to 4-5, the crowd went wild. The momentum was definitely behind Sue now, especially after Betty had lost her match point.

The Dutch player's serves were becoming more erratic and Sue needed to prove she could take the chance she had been given and hold her serve. The cheering was immense. 15-0, 15-15, 30-15, 30-30 (a quick reminder to ask spectators to stay silent during a rally) and then 30-40 – match point for the second time to Betty. She blew it again, her forehand finding the net. Deuce. Advantage Betty. And then, all of a sudden, it was Sue's forehand that found the net and everything was over. The collective sigh was audible. Sue lost the match and the chance to face Virginia in an all-British final. After an hour and three quarters of play, 'Neither player was on top form,' confirmed the commentator, but 'Sue will come again.'

Of course, Sue never did reach the semi-final again at the Championships, this being the furthest she ever got in the competition. She made no secret of the fact that she was too upset to watch Virginia play and win that year, spending the time shopping and spending a fortune instead. It was the final that was so close, yet so far. 'I can sum up my Wimbledon semi-final loss by saying I beat Betty Stöve three weeks later for the loss of one game,' she revealed. But the darling of Wimbledon did, as predicted, come back to SW19. Only this time she was carrying a microphone instead of her trusty wooden racket.

John McEnroe and Peter Fleming vs Brian Gottfried and Raúl Ramírez

Date: 7 July 1979
Score: 4-6, 6-4, 6-2, 6-2

'I thought doubles was a good way for me to practise and get some reps in – I didn't like to train in the gym as much as players these days.' John McEnroe

THEY SAY there is a moment in every tennis player's life when you need to make a mental decision to win or lose a game. Not that anyone chooses to lose a game, but you either make the choice to fight or make the choice to quit. Just such a moment came into the psyche of Peter Fleming in 1978, when he and his doubles partner, John McEnroe, faced Stan Smith and Bob Lutz in the second round of the tournament. They were two sets up before losing the next two to the veteran team and this was the point of do or die.

'These guys stink, how can we lose to these guys?' questioned a frustrated McEnroe to Fleming during the changeover. It was a light-bulb moment for Fleming. Their opponents were, until that point, well-respected figures in Peter's life. But through McEnroe's eyes, Peter was able to see that they were just, in fact, human – not unbeatable giants of the game – and that he and McEnroe were equally as good. 'My self-worth changed for all time,' he later confessed, and they beat Smith and Lutz in the final set.

McEnroe and Fleming didn't go on to win the title that year; they lost out to Bob Hewitt and Frew McMillan, 6-1, 6-4, 6-2, in the heaviest final defeat of the Championships since 1911. OK, so perhaps this was just a blip, and with fire reignited in their bellies, they entered the Men's Doubles competition in 1979. The odd couple, as they were often known (even Fleming once remarked that he was 'the big goon who played doubles with John McEnroe'), had joined forces in 1977 when Fleming picked out the loud, erratic, monstrously egocentric McEnroe to team up with. They became friends, playing junior tournaments in New York, and although their early matches weren't anything of particular note, when they reached Wimbledon they were ready to make their mark.

McEnroe had already come to the All England Club in 1977 in a bid to qualify for the tournament he had heard so much about. Not only did he win his way into the main draw, but he reached the semi-final stages, playing and then losing to the then 'bad boy' of tennis,

Jimmy Connors. He was just 17 years old and had played a record eight matches to get as far as he did. If this was the first time the All England Club had heard of John McEnroe, it certainly wasn't going to be the last. Peter Fleming, meanwhile, had made it into the top ten of the world rankings and was himself a formidable player – and, interestingly, a lot like his 'Superbrat' team-mate in more ways than first thought. Accepting that he had a terrible temper as a singles player, he never went past reaching No. 8 in the world, and put his losses down to not being able to control his anger. But partnered with John, unbelievably, there were relatively few outbursts or uncontrollable moments of frustration from either player. His most over-quoted statement – 'The greatest doubles pair in the world is John McEnroe and anyone!' – was, he reflected years later, more of an overstatement for dramatic purposes. There was no doubt that they were one of the best pairings on the circuit, complementing each other's style of play and personality.

Being the shorter of the pair, McEnroe chased every ball down, and when it was Fleming's turn to serve, he did it knowing that his partner would kill any return that came back. When they came to SW19 that year, they came as No. 1 seeds and their reputation was already formidable. They had a bit of an early-round wobble when they lost the first set to Australian qualifying duo, John Fitzgerald and Wayne Pascoe. When the Aussies took the first set from the No. 1 seeds, it was enough to kickstart a comeback. Knowing they had too much power to piddle around, McEnroe and Fleming went on to win the following three sets, 7-5, 6-2, 6-1. As their journey progressed to the final stages, the top seeds didn't need any more than three sets to win each match.

The stage for the final was set and the crowds were seated in the blazing summer sunshine, wondering if the young and feisty McEnroe and his tall, blond and athletic partner, Fleming, would continue the competition in the effortless style they had displayed so far. McEnroe hadn't made it past the fourth round that year in the Men's Singles competition, losing to fellow American, Tim Gullikson, in straight sets, while Fleming was relieved of his Singles challenge in the second round by Hank Pfister.

Both brought their singles skills to the doubles court and we never saw the tantrum-prone McEnroe, a sight we were used to witnessing when he played singles, when he played with his buddy. Of course, there might have been odd moments when Fleming had a quiet word in his younger partner's curly-hair-covered ear, but they were few and far between. 'I never told John to count to ten,' he admitted years later. 'He would probably have rammed a racket down on my head.' Indeed.

They went on to win 52 titles together, including seven Grand Slam wins. Four of those were on the grassy courts of Wimbledon – in 1979, 1981, 1983 and 1984. The final in 1979 was watched by an enthusiastic crowd who could see that the American gunslingers weren't just playing tennis as a business arrangement. There seemed to be a strong chemistry between them that allowed them to win that tournament and become a dominating force on the circuit over the next decade. You can't be serious? You bet we are.

Sister Act. Serena wins her first (of many) Wimbledon titles in 2002 after beating her big sister Venus.

Small but Mighty. A smiling Little Mo celebrates her first (of three) ladies' titles in her 1952 win against Louise Brough.

Over already? John Isner and Nicolas Mahut's three-day epic encounter finally comes to an end after 11 hours and five minutes.

Wave hello to the new Wimbledon Queen. Martina Navratilova looks sullen as Steffi Graf walks off court as the 1988 ladies champion.

A kiss for Althea. No hard feelings for Darlene as she congratulates Althea Gibson for becoming the first black woman to win the ladies' title.

Where are my parents? An emotional Pete Sampras embraces his dad after his 2000 win against Pat Rafter.

The summer of '69. Pancho Gonzales, the 'ageing lion', went through with a roar in his 112-game first-round match.

He's done it! Andy Murray breaks the British champion drought by winning the 2013 men's singles title.

Team USA. Jimmy Connors and Arthur Ashe are all smiles for the cameras in a no-love-lost final. Ashe won.

Ace? Roger that. Despite serving a punishing 25 aces, Federer lost out to Novak Djokovic in the 2019 men's final.

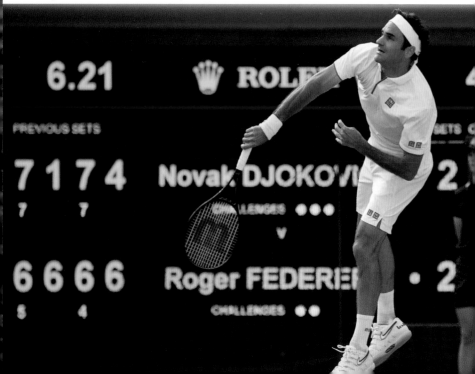

King doesn't get crowned. Billie Jean King loses out on the 1969 ladies' title to British champion Ann Jones.

Nadal's twilight win. The 2008 men's final saw Rafael Nadal beat Roger Federer in the last minutes of daylight.

Net Chris time. Evert loses in the 1978 ladies' final to Martina Navratilova, who was making her first appearance in the Championships final.

Emotional fall. Goran Ivanisevic wins the men's title in 2001 after battling it out against Pat Rafter.

45

Goran Ivanišević vs Pat Rafter

Date: 9 July 2001
Score: 6-3, 3-6, 6-3, 2-6, 9-7

'I don't care now if I ever win a match in my life again. Whatever I do in my life, wherever I go, I'm going to be always Wimbledon champion.' Goran Ivanišević

DUE TO the rain delays that caused the Men's semi-final between Tiger Tim and Goran Ivanišević (see Match 33) to be played over three days, 10,000 tickets were released on a first-come, first-served basis for the Men's final (or rather, the People's Monday match). Many fans had queued through the night to support the two finalists and, in a collective showing of respect, Centre Court played host to a rowdy, noisy, celebratory atmosphere – many in the crowd believing that both men deserved to win the trophy on their performances so far. Among the inflatable kangaroos and Australian flags were the painted faces of young Croats holding 'Go Goran!' posters. It was a unique display of energy and excitement and, for once, a Monday morning held more of a carnival atmosphere than the weekend that preceded it.

With support for both men at full capacity, those who had camped out for one of the unreserved seats were happy with a result either way. Both were old-timers, both were favourites, and both were loveable 'losers' who had reached the Wimbledon final before but never quite crossed the line. Rafter had lost to Sampras the year before, so many felt he deserved the trophy, while Ivanišević was 125th in the world when he came to Wimbledon and had shown the courage of a champion to get this far.

Ivanišević won the toss and opted to serve, his powerful serve-and-volley combo doing the business. He broke Rafter at the first attempt, which shook the Aussie (and the Australian cricket team who, having beaten England with a day to spare, were otherwise enjoying their time off). The Croatian continued to convert his powerful serves into points and took the first set 6-3. Not long after that, he lost the second set 3-6. In a tit-for-tat display, Rafter won the second set after asserting himself early on, breaking early thanks to two uncharacteristic double faults from Ivanišević.

As play got underway in the third set, the standard of tennis on display was ramped up tenfold. While Rafter was hunting down every ball with deft backhands and lunging volleys, Ivanišević's strong serves and court presence were a force to be reckoned with and, in the end, too much for Rafter, who lost the set 3-6.

The fourth set was all to play for. The shouts were louder, the flags were flung more furiously, and the energy from the crowd increased tenfold. The unique atmosphere was unlike anything the All England Club had seen before. At 3-2 up in the fourth the big Croatian was firing on all cylinders, but when he lost his service game point on a line call and Rafter broke him again after winning his own service game, Bad Goran was back – snarling at a line judge and taking his anger out on his racket. The match was now going to a final set. Would Ivanišević regain his composure? Would Rafter seek to exploit his irate opponent and cause him further upset? It was the sort of final every single person watching from the epicentre of tennis had been hoping for.

In the fifth set neither player wanted to lose their serve and, through pure grit and determination, they both held. At 3-3, Ivanišević served his 207th ace of that year's Championships, setting a new Wimbledon record. At 4-4 Rafter looked like he might get broken, but regained his composure. At 6-7, Ivanišević experienced the same feeling, but he too managed to claw back from 15-30 and two points from defeat.

At 7-7 in the final set, tension was high. One Australian fan had to leave her seat to take a breather. 'It was overwhelming,' she revealed. 'I couldn't bear to watch. I had my hands on my face a lot of the match, ready to cover my eyes, but I needed to come out.'

The noise was more like a football match or the crowd at a music concert, such was the excitement, the fun and the frivolity of this extra-time Monday extravaganza. At 7-7 and 15-40 down, Rafter tried a change of pace with his first serve, but it didn't work. Ivanišević smacked it back over the net to win the game.

Now at 8-7 and 40-15 up, Ivanišević was serving for the Championship. With a quick glance to the heavens, he knew he had to take this chance. It was now or never. But wait … a double fault. That's OK though. No one double-faults twice in a row at match point. And yet … double fault. The crowd went from cheering to groaning to shouting all in one breath. If there were any nerves left, they were well and truly shredded. Winning the advantage, Goran was at match point again and the crowd were going wild.

His first serve went out and, as he shaped to serve once more, you could hear a pin drop. The second serve carried pressure in its 109mph flight and he ran into the net, ready to volley a return. But he didn't need to. His serve was too strong and Rafter's backhand return dropped into the net. The whole of Centre Court erupted in a collective cheer, having been part of three hours of drama, anxiety and emotion. Ivanišević was overcome with emotion and fell to his knees in relief, such was the intensity of his euphoria, before both players hugged at the net. There was no clear winner that day. Ivanišević was the one holding aloft the trophy, but the spectators who had been lucky enough to witness this history-making final surely felt they had a hand on the prize too.

46

Mansour Bahrami and Henri Leconte vs Jacco Eltingh and Paul Haarhuis

Date: 11 July 2015
Score: 4-6, 5-7

'When the crowds laugh, I am the happiest man in the whole world.' Mansour Bahrami

YOU ARE going to have to forgive a little indulgence here. There are many doubles games that could have taken this slot, but none of them would bring you the magical maverick himself, Mansour Bahrami. If you like your tennis with a slice of farce, a whiff of pantomime and a dollop of jaw-drop drop shots (try saying that after a couple of Pimm's), not to mention rallies that end in a shot being caught in the pocket of an Iranian's shorts, you'll be well aware of the legendary Bahrami. And no, we don't use the word legendary lightly.

The irony behind Bahrami's most audacious and entertaining displays of theatrical tennis is that he could have been – had he not been born in a country where tennis was banned – a top-seeded player. To cut a long story short, growing up in Iran he showed great potential in the sport and, at the age of 13, it was whispered that he could potentially become one of the country's greatest players. But then Islamic fundamentalist leader, the Ayatollah Khomeini, banned tennis and Bahrami wasn't allowed to pick up a racket until a connection was made to the foreign minister to grant him a visa to visit France. But even then he didn't play for several years for fear of being deported, because his visa had run out and he didn't want to claim political asylum. It wasn't until he started entering a few low-key tennis tournaments to win a little money that interest in him as a player grew, and it wasn't until he was 30 years old that he joined the Association of Tennis Professionals (ATP) as a proper player. By then, for most professional tennis players, the glory days were over. He started to play in doubles tournaments, to some degree of success. But getting bums on seats to watch you play was one thing; Bahrami was all about putting smiles on faces. And that he did, time after time, tournament after tournament.

And so to the match of 2015 at SW19, the Senior Gentlemen's Invitation Doubles (for players aged 45 years and over), featuring Henri Leconte and Bahrami against Jacco Eltingh and Paul Haarhuis. Coincidentally, Bahrami was the oldest player in that year's tournament, at 59 years old. Alongside the Invitation Doubles, these games rank high on most fans' wish list as a chance to watch some of the legends of yesteryear proving they still have what it takes. But really, none of them takes it that seriously. This is a chance to see former legends in a more relaxed setting, although some former big names of the game choose to finish on the high of their glory days rather than return to play in this round-robin format of eight pairs.

The outside courts are always the stage for these matches and, together with a particularly devilish Henri Leconte, the afternoon's entertainment was set. Losing in the first set 5-2, Leconte decided to have a little fun during the break of play, interacting with the crowd and questioning why the ball boy was holding an umbrella for shade for Eltingh and Haarhuis, which he described as 'crazy' in this country (he had a point, during Wimbledon the sun should always be the most celebrated guest). He then took off one of the umpire's shoes and threw it into the crowd. As you do.

As they went out to play with the shoe returned and normal (ish) service resumed, it seemed Bahrami and Leconte were ready for a bit of mischief, having been (semi) serious for the first 20 minutes of the game. When Bahrami served and volleyed the return back over the net, the next rally was pure entertainment. Leconte and Eltingh hit the ball to each other, back and forth over the net, for 13 volleys before, realising they were just standing there waiting and looking rather surplus to requirements, Bahrami decided to have his own volley rally at the net and started hitting to Haarhuis. The crowd were in hysterics. Balls were being hit across each other until Leconte and Eltingh, now getting a little tired of their ever-lasting volleying, moved even closer to the net to tap the ball over to each other and not exert too much effort. It was showmanship at its best. The fans milling around the edges of the outside courts, hearing the sounds of a delighted crowd, hung out by the gates to wait for a vacated seat. In the end, the point went to Leconte and Bahrami after a cheeky little shot finished the rally and the applause took over.

If this was a pantomime, you'd be booing the umpires and cheering the players and the slow clapping would build to a crescendo that would give Bahrami the rhythm he needed to do a little dance and, even though the comedy duo didn't win, they did in fact lose to the eventual winners, 4-6, 5-7, and no one fractured a hip. Which surely counts for something. One fan who watched the game that day suggested that the comedy combination of Bahrami and Leconte should be bottled up and served with a Pimm's and punnet of strawberries to reflect the joy they bring to the All England Club. We couldn't agree more.

John Isner vs Nicolas Mahut

Date: 24 June, 25 June, 26 June 2010
Score: 6-4, 3-6, 6-7, 7-6, 70-68

'What can I say, the guy's an absolute
warrior. It stinks that someone has to lose.'
John Isner

MOST OUTSIDE courts have the odd moment of magic that lives in the minds of spectators for the tournament, fading away as the Championships wrap up and nothing more than a blur as the summer months play on. But not this game. Not this year. Not this outside court, which is now forever adorned with a blue plaque to mark the history that was made there in 2010.

'We all knew something unusual was occurring. The crowds were building up around the court as the match progressed,' said one visitor to Wimbledon on Wednesday, day two of the match.

Court 18 is overlooked on one side by the roof of the Media Centre, where many of the overseas broadcasters have their 'stand up' presenting positions. As the spectacle unfolded, more television staff flocked to view a piece of history in action.

By day three of the match, the crowd on the roof had grown three deep, which was 'unheard of' confirmed a TV director, 'considering most of us have watched more tennis than you could ever care to do. Yet it drew you in, something magnetic about knowing it must end soon and what would the reaction be when it did.'

The BBC commentators for the game were equally bemused by how this match was developing. Former Wimbledon favourite Greg Rusedski was alongside newbie Ron McIntosh, who was on his first tennis match commentary stint. Ever since then, the general joke is for the TV director to see who is commentating on the match and, knowing if it's Ron, there will be some banter about him being the kiss of death. But back to the game.

The first day of play certainly didn't give any indication that this match was going to be anything other than a low-key affair, and both players took a relatively straightforward set each before qualifier Mahut took the third. The afternoon crowd were then treated to a fourth-set tie-break that saw Isner, in a shout of triumph, go one point away from winning the fourth set to square the match at two sets all. Shouts of support and standing ovations were the order of the day as the American aced his French opponent and, after three hours of play, the match was level. But it was 9.10pm and the umpire had to make the unpopular decision to suspend play until the next day. Coming back fresh on Wednesday afternoon, the players were keen to get the final set completed so that the victor could enjoy some rest and practice time before the next round. How funny. The best-laid plans, eh?

As the set went to 6-6, the players weren't giving an inch. The game count was slowly creeping up as the quality levels remained equally impressive. Serving at 9-10 and 30-30, there was a chance for Mahut to be broken and lose the match when he doubled-faulted. But then he pulled out an aggressive ace and the play went back to deuce. Mahut took his service game and the play was level again after Isner failed to put any pressure on Mahut's weaker second serve. That had been a vital chance for Isner and, as Greg pointed out, could prove to be a costly mistake for the American. The play went on and on. The American and the Frenchman equalled each other in ability and technique. The bullet-for-bullet serves, the balanced returns, the equal athleticism were all key to understanding why this match was like no other. No one comes to Wimbledon wanting to play second best, and these players didn't give an inch to each other. There was no comeback or whitewash, it was purely tit for tat.

The roof of the Media Centre, which has a great viewing platform for Court 18, was filling up. One former TV director was perplexed at the numbers he was seeing on the scoreboard. 'I was looking at the scores, it was something like 20 games to 19, and I was left wondering what had gone wrong with the scoreboard because that couldn't possibly be right,' he pondered. It was.

The seated spectators were in no hurry to speed things up as they basked in the glorious sunshine with a sporting show unfolding in front of them and, as the day went on, the match went on … and on. The crowds had grown and people were filling all the gaps to get a glimpse of the action on court, waiting for the spectacle to end. But it simply didn't. When Mahut stood to serve at 32-33, there was little sign that either player was tiring. Mahut was firing out some sharp serves while Isner was moving quickly around the court. There were a few moments of stretching and flexing from the tall American, in a bid to check his body was still up for the challenge after hours in the sun.

After a tremendous return down the tramline, Isner had two match points in the bag as Mahut served at 15-40. The first serve went out and many believed this was now the crucial point. Mahut's second serves had been slower and all Isner needed to do was take this advantage. But he couldn't and Mahut only had one more match point to escape if he wanted to level the fifth set at 33-33. He fired an ace that Isner could not return, play went to deuce and then advantage Mahut, and then another unreturnable serve brought the games back level.

After 99 games there was still no sign of anyone crossing the finishing line. It was too much for the electronic scoreboards; they stopped working. Now Mahut was serving in the 100th game of the set and the crowd were starting to get more vocal and distracting – although that didn't stop Mahut pulling out his 77th ace of the match as he went 30-0 ahead, then 40-0, and then the 100th game was won. Fifty games apiece and so far this set had been played for over four hours. The crowds stood to acknowledge this astonishing set and these astonishing players.

Surely, many thought, surely they would tire soon and the slightly less exhausted man would crawl over the finish line. But, still smiling, the players played on. At 58-59 Mahut still had the energy to power over aces; 15-15, 30-15 ... the last drops of evening sun had dropped away from the court ... 40-30 and Isner pummelled back a return to bring it to deuce. He was going for broke, and when Mahut double-faulted to give Isner another match point, the cheers and shouts around the court sounded almost as exhausted as the players were now looking. Surely Mahut wouldn't have the energy to pull out another winning serve? Even though he looked like he was moving on autopilot, he did just that and smashed out his 95th ace.

'This match is never going to end at this rate,' acknowledged Greg. The mental strength of both players was astounding as they took encouragement from the crowds, but as Isner hit a long return to give Mahut the advantage, it was another game all done. At 59 games apiece Mahut approached the umpire's chair to question the fading light. Isner was happy to carry on, but play was suspended. Mahut was desperate to get away. After exactly ten hours of match play, no one could really blame him. The action, the tension, the relentlessness ... everyone was tired.

By the time the players returned to Court 18 on Thursday afternoon, they were famous. They walked over to the court from the dressing rooms through a throng of people wanting to take photos and cheer on these two unlikely heroes, and everyone was fascinated as to what would unfold on the third day of play in this remarkable match. Fresh, determined and welcomed onto court with a standing ovation from those lucky enough to get a Court 18 seat, the players prepared to continue this now historic match.

After another hour of play, it was beginning to look like Greg's words would ring true: how and when would this ever end? At 68-69 Mahut's serve was back with full force but, following a night's rest, Isner's returns were just as formidable and a drop-shot response put him 15-30 ahead.

Mahut levelled at 30-30, but Isner went ahead with a well-placed forehand that set up his fifth match point.

But we'd been here before, several hours and several games ago, only this time there was a real chance for Isner, in taking his time, to play a blistering backhand to win the game. He did it, and the enormity of the situation crashed down on him as he fell to the ground in relief, arms and legs in the air. The cheer from the crowds watching all around Wimbledon rose to a level normally reserved for Championship-winning moments. Still in a state of shock, Isner took a standing ovation from the crowd and clapped them in return. The resolve of Mahut had finally been broken. John McEnroe and Tracy Austin had dropped by to watch and stood to clap the players as they accepted special mementoes of their record-breaking marathon. At long last there was now a winner of this epic encounter. The fifth set alone lasted over eight hours, longer than any tennis match in history. The whole match lasted 11 hours and five minutes and a record-breaking 216 aces were served. It was definitely time for a lie-down.

48

Billie Jean King and Owen Davidson vs Raúl Ramírez and Janet Newberry

Date: 8 July 1973
Score: 6-3, 6-2

*'Owen made every first volley when I played
mixed with him, he would hit that funny
little spin serve and get right in and I swear
he made 99% of his first volleys, and when
you do that, you're up there together at the
net. We both love the net.'* Billie Jean King

IT WAS a match made in heaven when Australian Owen Davidson and Billie Jean King took to the court – they were formidable opponents for any mixed doubles title contenders. They won the Championship title four times – in 1967, 1971, 1973 and 1974 – and collected eight Grand Slam mixed doubles titles in total. For singles champion Billie, playing in the doubles and mixed doubles was equally as important as flying solo, and this Mixed Doubles final certainly proved her level of dedication.

Owen and Billie, having secured two Mixed Doubles titles by this point, had the ability to bring the complete package to their game. Left-handed Owen had a punishing serve that few female opponents could return easily, and if they did, they then found Billie waiting at the net. She was a fearless competitor and loved to attack, which in turn gave Owen confidence; he admitted he lacked a little self-confidence in his singles games.

In the summer of 1973 – coincidentally the year Billie won the monumental Battle of The Sexes tennis game against former No. 1 Bobby Rigg (but that's a whole other book) – bad weather had upset proceedings and the Ladies' Singles final had not been played on the Friday as planned. So it was on this Saturday that Billie won the Ladies' Singles title, beating Chris Evert 6-0, 7-5 and giving her a fifth Wimbledon title. She then joined forces with fellow American, Rosemary Casals, to take part in the Ladies' Doubles semi-final match against Evonne Goolagong and Janet Young, winning 7-5, 7-5. And if that wasn't enough, she also took part in the Ladies' Doubles final, going head-to-head with her former doubles partner, Betty Stöve, and her new partner, Françoise Dürr. Billie and Rosemary won that too. She was on her way to becoming the first player of the Open Era to claim the Triple Crown, but she would need to play and win another three matches the following day if that achievement was to be reached. And there was always time for practice too. While Owen waited in the changing rooms, a call came through at 7pm to tell him that Billie was out on No. 2 Court and waiting for him to come and play.

With three games of the Mixed Doubles still to be decided, Wimbledon opened its gates to the public on the Sunday, the day after the Championships normally finished. With play now extended for an extra day, and fans eager to make the most of the bonus tennis action on offer, the quarter-final match of Billie and Owen up against Jan Kodeš and Martina Navratilova was up first. It was a straightforward 6-3, 6-0 victory and Owen and Billie marched on to the semi-final, a match against Alex Metreveli and Olga Morozova.

This was perhaps the first time their chances of winning were in doubt. In the quarter-final they had only dropped three games, but now they were a set down and in the second set giving it all they'd got to stay. They went on to take the second set and clinched the win, dropping just one game in the third and final set. But with this three-set victory (5-7, 7-5, 1-6) and still one more match to win before they could celebrate the title, this was tiring work.

Encouraged by an enthusiastic Centre Court crowd, not to mention the chance to win the Triple Crown, Billie gave it all she had, showing such competitive spirit and aggression – together with Owen's penetrating volleys –

that the pair were too good for Raúl Ramírez and Janet Newberry. After winning the first set 6-3, they dropped only two games in the second set to win the Mixed Doubles title.

It was an epic display of athleticism and endurance by Billie. She played six matches in two days across three competitions and won them all. She made the decision to send her husband in her place to the winners' ball that Saturday night, opting instead for an early night. It's worth bearing in mind next time you think you have a busy weekend ...

49

Ken Rosewall vs Cliff Richey

Date: 29 June 1971
Score: 6-8, 5-7, 6-4, 9-7, 7-5

*'If I were asked to name one aspect of tennis
that is the biggest weakness of players of all
levels, I would probably say concentration.
However good your shots, all is lost if the
mind is not controlling every move.'*

Ken Rosewall

ON PAPER, the result for this quarter-final will simply say that Rosewall defeated Richey and progressed to the semi-final stage of the Championships. But that basic summary does nothing to describe the four-hour battle that was fought on Centre Court between these two doggedly determined athletes.

Thirty-six-year-old Ken Rosewall was making a bid for his fourth Wimbledon final appearance. Many commentators believed, having been denied the title three times before, that this would be his year. After a 17-year stretch at the All England Club he was certainly a familiar face, so it wasn't surprising that the No. 3 seed was an old crowd favourite. But standing in his way in this quarter-final contest was the 24-year-old American No. 1, Cliff Richey. And stand in his way he did. No one was quite expecting the levels of determination Richey showed to take the first two sets in the manner he did. The level of play was heightened beyond measure as the near-veteran Australian and young Texan fought in a match that one newspaper described as 'cruel in its demands upon the mental and physical reserves of both men'.

The scores for each set certainly tell an interesting tale. Rosewall began his campaign with the confidence and poise of a man who felt at ease on grass, but he did perhaps slightly underestimate his opponent. Richey was aggressive in his shots, took the chances to break at the right time and attacked with purpose. Both men were working physically hard across every inch of their majestic stage, chasing down shots to strike and riposte. Mistakes were made at vital stages too; a double fault by Rosewall allowed Richey to break and take the second set. Richey himself had 11 foot faults called against him. When the Texan No. 6 seed took the first two sets and continued his onslaught to go 4-2 up in the third and love-30 on Rosewall's serve, there was a sense that this was too much of an uphill battle for the Australian. He had fought in vain so far; surely any counterattack at this stage was asking far too much from a man 12 years older than his opponent who was firing on all cylinders.

What the crowds were about to witness was a masterclass in resilience and defiance, in technique and unfazed attitude in the face of defeat. Rosewall's body was chest-deep in a losing abyss, but his racket was reaching for the stars. And it was in the third set that the tide turned. Richey had failed to convert his lead and Rosewall had fought back to go 5-4 ahead. After a quick break at the umpire's chair, Rosewall bent down and pulled up both of his socks. It was a gesture that was to have symbolic significance. When Richey double-faulted on his serve, Rosewall was at last able to claim a set and show the youngster that the battle had only just begun.

Rosewall was riding into battle with renewed vigour, unruffled at still being a set behind and ready to fire up his racket. Equally, Richey rose to the challenge and went 7-6 ahead in the fourth set with a serve to come. But he couldn't quite finish the job and, after three hours and seven minutes of play, the match was level – a situation that seemed impossible only a short time ago. They were two sets apiece and the physical and mental exhaustion was no match for each man's raw determination.

The top dog had gone under, but he was by no means out. The growing number of fans gathered around Centre Court added to the inferno of sound as the fifth set got underway. Each time they changed ends, the crowd roared in support, knowing it would be the more courageous character that would be victorious. Not that either was lacking courage; this was about who was tougher.

For a while both were worthy of that title. Rosewall managed to recover from 15-40 down to go 5-4 ahead, with Richey serving to stay in the match. That was one of five break points that Richey was unable to convert, adding to the story of this remarkable match. Add in too that Richey was one point from defeat on four occasions in that game, but with a leaping smash and fireball volley was able to save Championship point four times.

The crowd were exhausted by what they were witnessing. This was all about which of the players had one last spark of fight left in them. In the 12th game Rosewall was 6-5 ahead and, after managing to recover from 15-40 down, set himself up with another Championship point thanks to a forehand volley powered beyond Richey. It was a simple backhand strike that eventually gave Rosewall victory. As every single person rose from their seat in an eruption of cheers, claps and shouts of relief, Centre Court celebrated the hearts and minds of both players who had put on such a courageous display.

Rosewall acknowledged the victory by simply holding his racket aloft for a few seconds, humble in the victory and the knowledge that this had been a match full of strength of character from both sides. For Richey, this would be as far as he would ever get in the Championships.

He managed to reach the semi-final of another Grand Slam tournament the following year, the US Open, but lost to Arthur Ashe in straight sets.

50

Lleyton Hewitt vs David Nalbandian

Date: 7 July 2002
Score: 6-1, 6-3, 6-2

*'It's a real ripper, I had to look up to
the scoreboard to see if it was real.'*
Lleyton Hewitt

IN ONE of the most one-sided Men's finals of the Open
Era, No. 1 seed Lleyton Hewitt pretty much came, saw
and conquered his opponent in the same manner he had
played all tournament. He had only dropped two sets
on his journey to the final, losing both of those in his
quarter-final clash with Sjeng Schalken, whom he beat
6-2, 6-2, 6-7, 1-6, 7-5. It was a test of nerve for the top
seed to be able to pull himself back from the hole he had
dug for himself when he squandered four match points
in the third set. But pull himself back he did and, sadly
for us Brits, he also saw off Tiger Tim in the semi-final
(the fourth time in five years that Tim had the door to
the final slammed in his face).

This was the 116th edition of the Championships and it was turning out to be a strange affair. The defending champion, Goran Ivanišević, wasn't here to defend his title due to injury and so Lleyton was asked if he'd like to play his opening match on Centre Court (he declined, worried that the grass might be too 'glassy'), while the likes of Pete Sampras, Andre Agassi and Roger Federer were all knocked out in the early rounds. In fact, of the top 17 seeded players only Tim and Lleyton made it past the fourth round.

But how boring would the world of Wimbledon be if we only ever saw the top seeds reaching the final stages? It's much more fun for the underdog to go forth and that's pretty much what happened here. No. 28 seed David Nalbandian from Argentina was playing his first Men's tournament at Wimbledon and had never played on Centre Court before. To help him deal with that monumental debut, he was allowed to practise on the hallowed turf before the final. Not that it really did much good, but that's beside the point – at Wimbledon, everyone is treated fairly.

Still, the practice hits on the grand stage probably didn't prepare him for the 15,000 pairs of eyes that greeted him as he walked out on the day of the final, a dull and mizzly afternoon with rain lurking overhead. The Australian player was, in contrast, very much at ease here; he loved Wimbledon and the fans loved him. And having not seen an Aussie win the title since Pat Cash in 1987, Centre Court and those gathered on Henman Hill and around the grounds were ready to cheer on both finalists in a good-natured way – even if they were secretly hoping for more of a fight from Nalbandian.

Sadly, a double fault on his very first point showed how nervous he was, so the crowd, in true spirit-raising fashion, made it their mission to cheer every point he won from then on. Lleyton was on top form and showing exactly why he was the World No. 1. He owned the baseline with his powerful strokes, attacking like his life was on the line, and after breaking his opponent in that first game he went on to win the first set in 33 minutes.

Nalbandian was finally able to apply some pressure when, in the sixth game, he earned two break points after Hewitt smashed two balls into the net. And he certainly showed some fight when he threw himself at full stretch (in the manner of Becker) across the court to hit a diving volley and save a set point.

In the second set Nalbandian had two break points in the first game, but he sent two forehand drives wide of the mark, giving Lleyton the first game of the second set. If he was wishing for rain to give himself chance to regroup, he was granted that wish when, after an appeal to the umpire, Mike Morrissey, play was suspended. The drizzle that had hung heavy in the air was turning heavier and it was decided that a short rain break was in order.

They were off court for a short 15-minute rain break, but it wasn't the weather that delayed play after that. A few minutes after the covers came off, so too did the clothes of a spectator who decided that now was the optimal time to streak on court. 'I never go on during play, it's against my ethics,' confirmed streaker Mark Roberts. 'But then rain stopped play and things got a bit disorganised, so I ran down the steps, jumped over the wall, took my clothes off and ran on. Everyone cheered, even the Royal Box. I did a few somersaults and a moonwalk and then dived over the net.'

The crowd were certainly entertained, and when he feigned being caught before making a run for it and somersaulting over the net, the players were equally bemused. He was caught and led off, and the players were able to continue their match. Ahh well, if this wasn't to be a tense final to keep us on the edge of our seats, at least it was memorable for other reasons. New balls please!

The top seed, unfazed by the nudity, went on to break Nalbandian in the next game to go 2-0 up, but then, in a few minutes of brilliance, the Argentinian broke back after a terrific rally and lob volley won him his first break game. He won the next game too, holding his serve and his nerve by mirroring the style that Hewitt was showing – two-handed, tight-angled powerful backhands and whipping forehand passes.

The games were now equal at 3-3 and, at 30-30 in the seventh game, it looked like perhaps there might be more to this final than suspected … but then the rain came again and the players scampered off. After the 34-minute delay it was Lleyton that came back firing and ready to get things wrapped up, and he took the second set with a game-winning ace. The second set was over in 43 minutes; Hewitt was slacking.

Turning his attention to the third (and, he hoped, final) set, Hewitt was fired up. He was going for every shot, relentlessly and aggressively, until he broke Nalbandian. Sensing he was on course for victory, he let out a yell of enthusiasm to the crowd and players' box. It wasn't all over yet though. In a brave last stand, Nalbandian broke back and the crowd roared their enthusiasm. But all thoughts of a comeback to end all comebacks were short-lived and, after disputing a line call that he believed to be unfair, he seemed to deflate on the spot and all confidence was gone.

Hewitt won his serve, broke again and, now serving for the Championship, it was just a matter of time; 15-0, 30-0, 40-0 and that was it. The game was done, the match was won. Hewitt fell to his knees in relief and euphoria, and the crowd celebrated a worthy champion.

Had they been aware that this was to be the last time they would see him in a Wimbledon final, perhaps they might have given him more than the customary acknowledgement. As they stood and clapped their new champion, few would have believed that this would be the 21-year-old's last Grand Slam title. For someone who admitted he had a 'never say die' attitude, he was never quite able to repeat the success he had that year. But winning a Wimbledon title (even if it is your only one) meant that he earned membership to the All England Club, and that is something that meant more to him than a trophy. 'It's the home of tennis, I get goosebumps walking into this place. That's something I can always come back and enjoy over the years.' Indeed you can, Lleyton, indeed you can.

Bibliography

Barrett, J., *Wimbledon: The Official History*, (Kingston-Upon-Thames, Vision Sports Publishing, 2020 (5th ed.)).

Hewitt, I., *Centre Court: The Jewel in Wimbledon's Crown*, (Kingston-Upon-Thames ,Vision Sports Publishing, 2016 (3rd ed.)).

Parsons, J., *The Ultimate Encyclopedia of Tennis*, (London: Hodder & Stoughton, 1998)

www.atptour.com

www.bbc.co.uk/sport

www.britishnewspaperarchive.co.uk

www.dailymail.co.uk/sport/tennis

www.espn.com/tennis

www.gq-magazine.co.uk

www.hearldscotland.com

www.independent.co.uk/sport/tennis

www.latimes.com

www.liverpoolecho.co.uk

www.tennis365.com

www.tennisworldusa.org

www.theguardian.com/sport

www.thetimes.co.uk

www.washingtonpost.com

www.wimbledon.com

Also available at all good book stores

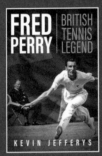

9781785312908

9781785315169

9781785313837

9781785316364

9781785313868